THE LOVE TEACHINGS OF
Kama Sutra

Krishna watching Radha at her bath. Opaque water
colour on paper. Garhwal, Panjab Hills, c 1800

THE LOVE TEACHINGS OF
Kama Sutra

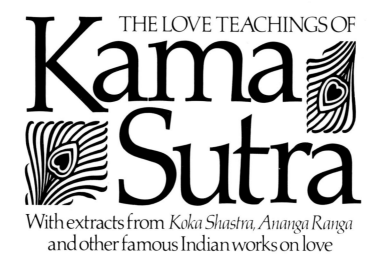

With extracts from *Koka Shastra, Ananga Ranga*
and other famous Indian works on love

Translated from Sanskrit originals by Indra Sinha

MARLOWE & COMPANY
New York

To Vickie, my wife.

Designed and produced by Nicholas Enterprises Ltd
28 Percy Street, London W1P 0LD

First North American Edition, 1997
Marlowe & Company
632 Broadway, Seventh Floor
New York, New York, 10012

Design consultant: Nigel Soper, Millons, London

ISBN 1-56924-779-X

Library of Congress Cataloging-in-Publication Data
available upon request from the publisher

Printed in Belgium

श्रीगणेशायनमः

In the name of Lord Ganesh

CONTENTS

INTRODUCTION

With the probable exception of *svastika*, no two Sanskrit words are more widely known and misunderstood than *Kama Sutra*. In the West the work is commonly believed to be a salacious, anecdotal account of exotic lovemaking, yet in India it is often given to young brides to read before their weddings. My own introduction to it was when, at a boarding school in the Rajasthan desert, a bearded, turbanned college-servant smuggled in a poorly-printed copy of the Burton translation for a friend who had heard that it was a 'hot book'. I can still remember our boredom and disappointment.

Kama Sutra contains no anecdotes and is very far from being merely a sex manual. Only one book of its seven deals with the techniques of physical lovemaking. The rest cover subjects as diverse as how to furnish and decorate a house, how to woo a bride, how husbands and wives are to behave to one another, how religious festivals are to be celebrated, the kitchen provisioned and the garden planted. *Kama Sutra* is an attempt, the earliest extant, to define the whole relationship between a man and a woman.

At the heart of this relationship, of course, is the sexual act. The questions *Kama Sutra* sets out to answer are: with whom should this act be performed, under what circumstances should it be performed, and how should it be performed? The approach, therefore, is that of a *shastra*, or scientific text, which is why it was composed in *sutras*, or aphorisms. Panini's great grammar, Kautilya's *Arthashastra* and Patanjali's yoga teachings were also composed in *sutras*.

Kama, which is the name of the Hindu god of love, means 'pleasure'. Not just sexual pleasure, but any pleasure which can be experienced through the senses, for instance sniffing a rose or listening to music. *Kama Sutra* itself defines the term thus:

> *Kama* is the delight of body, mind and soul
> in exquisite sensation;
> awaken eyes, nose, tongue, ears and skin,
> and between sense and sensed,
> the essence of *Kama* will flower.

Kama Sutra can thus be translated as 'Aphorisms on Pleasure'.

The work was composed by Mallanaga Vatsyayana, some time between the second and fifth centuries AD. My own inclination is to place Vatsyayana in the middle of the fourth century, during the reign of the Gupta emperor Samudragupta, but the question is unresolved. We know nothing of the author beyond what he tells us himself: that he was a celibate *yogi* who had attained *samadhi*, which might vulgarly be translated as enlightenment. In his day he was perhaps as famous a teacher as are, for instance, Bhagwan Shree Rajneesh or Maharishi Mahesh Yogi today (indeed Vatsyayana has been called Maharishi in India for centuries). He himself states quite clearly that the work was not written for any motive, other than to enable people to understand *Kama* and to use and enjoy it properly.

Kama is one of the three great aims of Hindu life, but it must always be pursued in harmony with the other two, *Dharma* and *Artha*. These terms have no English equivalents, but are crucial to the understanding of *Kama Sutra*. *Dharma*, from the Sanskrit root *dhru*, 'to hold', is religious, moral and social duty. It means acting in accordance with religious teachings, the laws of society and one's own conscience and nature. It is a duty determined, as much as anything, by sex, caste and status, and is therefore not the same for everyone. The warrior's *Dharma*, as Lord Krishna told Arjuna in *Bhagavad-Gita*, is to fight and kill; the priest's is to bless and make sacrifices; the labourer's is to labour, and the courtesan's is to give pleasure to her clients. By fulfilling one's *Dharma*, so the belief goes, one is freed from the accumulated sins of one's past lives and from the cycle of life and death.

Artha is simpler – the duty to amass wealth and possessions for the benefit of one's family. It is interesting to note that learning and craft-skills are considered part of *Artha*. The practice of *Artha* must always be tempered by *Dharma*, otherwise it is sheer opportunism. Kautilya, in his *Arthashastra* ('The Science of Artha') often out-Machiavellis Machiavelli. *Kama*, *Artha* and *Dharma* are to be pursued in harmony, no one overshadowing the other two. They are inextricably bound together and each, practised properly, must benefit the other two. In *Bhagavad-Gita* Lord Krishna says: 'I am that *Kama* which is consonant with *Dharma*.' It is the *Dharma* of a married man to make love to his wife, and if there is merit to be gained from doing something, there is more merit to be gained from doing it well. No wonder then that *Kama Sutra* and the medieval love texts are so prodigiously detailed, written to create connoisseurs of sensuality; it is all part of *Dharma*.

This is why the house is to be filled with flowers, scented with perfumes, decorated with objects to delight the eye, attended by skilled singers, dancers and musicians, furnished with the softest rugs and pillows. Only the most delicious foods and wines are to be served at parties, only the most beautiful clothes worn, and the conversation is always to sparkle with wit. So with lovemaking. The lists of techniques provide sensations which can be chosen and savoured like delicacies from a gourmet menu. This need not be as contrived and unspontaneous as it sounds. We could regard the techniques as a grammar of love that has to be mastered before one can express oneself with fluency and felicity. Or, more aptly perhaps, as five finger exercises in *raga* and *tala* which need practising before music can be made. Indeed, the reason I have included so many positions from the medieval texts is to illustrate the way lovemaking should flow, like a *raga* played by an Indian *ustad*, from one perfectly executed figure to the next, improvised but effortless.

In *hatha-yoga* also, and in the dance, we encounter positions (also called *asanas*) which are held for a few moments and which then flow into the next. We know that Bharata's *Natyashastra*, the seminal work on Indian dance, profoundly influenced at least the medieval writers on love, but the relationship between *hatha-yoga* and the love texts has never been sufficiently explored. They have in common that they call their physical exercises *asanas* and *bandhas*; Vatsyayana cites *Padmasana* (the Lotus Posture), the most famous of all *yoga* postures, as one of his positions. And dozens of the medieval lovemaking postures are clearly *yoga*-derived. But it is only with the development of *tantra* that the *yoga* disciplines of posture and breath-control are at last combined with sexual practices in the service of meditation and to unite the worshipper with the cosmic energy, or *shakti*, symbolized by the great goddess.

The earliest *tantra* texts of the Shakta school are said to have been written in about the seventh century AD, but the tradition, even today, is largely oral, and according to one authority at least was already well-developed in the time of the Guptas, which is where I place Vatsyayana. In its earliest forms, it dates back to Vedic times. A shadowy work quoted in the *Chandogya Upanishad* (*c.* 800 BC) is the *Vamadevya*, 'a song concerned with sexual congress', which compares the sexual act to a religious sacrifice, identifying each stage with a corresponding stage in the ritual. And the oldest of the *Upanishads* (the early commentaries on the *Vedas*, the *Brihadaranyaka*, says:

> Woman is the sacrificial fire,
> the lips of her *yoni* the fuel,
> the hairs around them the smoke,
> and the vagina itself the flame.
> The act of penetration is the lighting,
> the feelings of pleasure are the sparks.
> In this fire the gods offer up semen-seed,
> and from this offering man is born.

The teacher of this doctrine was the *guru* of Svetaketu Auddalaki, whom Vatsyayana claims as one of his own predecessors.

Could Vatsyayana have been aware of an oral *tantric* tradition when he wrote *Kama Sutra*? One place where a covert reference may be intended is a *sutra* towards the end of Book II, Compatibility, in which he gives a list of what appear to be synonyms and euphemisms for the sexual act. The order in which these occur suggests two sequences, first the physical chain reaction which is to be harnessed, and second, the techniques to be used in a religious ritual analogous to the secret ritual of the *tantras*. There is no other logical reason why the list should appear in this place, or indeed at all, and it is followed by the cryptic statement that 'people of intelligence and sensitivity will find these remarks sufficient'. My interpretation of the relevant *sutra* (II 1: 32 in the Chaukamba text) will be found on page 44. Of the medieval texts, *Ratiratnapradipika* is particularly full of references to *tantra* and actually gives a posture which it attributes to the Kaula *tantrics*, who used ritualized intercourse in their worship. These speculations should not, perhaps, be taken very seriously. I have laboured the point precisely because the relationship of *Kama Sutra* to *hatha-yoga* and *tantra* remains so unclear. Perhaps some scholar will be goaded to research. It is certainly beyond question that Vatsyayana's main objective is not to retail mysticism, but simply to maximize the pleasure that men and women can get from lovemaking, and to chronicle sexual practice as it existed in his day.

Although he wrote nearly two thousand years ago, Vatsyayana's chapters on the techniques of lovemaking and seduction seem uncannily modern. He attacks the old belief, propounded by Auddalaki some eleven hundred years before him, that there is no such thing as a female orgasm, and goes further, to say that men should always consider women's pleasure before their own. The absurd belief that penis-size has anything to do with satisfying a lover is dimissed in the very enlightened section on compatibility. Physical proportions and sexual temperaments may cause mismatches, but these can be compensated for by learning and applying the various love techniques. There are few aberrations of belief or logic to disturb the modern reader and, since human psychology and physiology have not altered in the slightest since *Kama Sutra* was written, it remains as valuable a manual of lovemaking technique today as it was when it was written.

Vatsyayana's work, as he himself tells us, was the culmination of a long tradition, which begins with Prajapati, the Creator of Mankind, who first gave the love teachings in order to teach men and women how to lead satisfying, moral lives. The teachings were passed on by Nandi, who is the bull-guardian of the god Shiva's palace. Legend has it that when Shiva and his wife Parvati were locked away making love for a thousand years, Nandi was inspired to utter the *Kama* teachings, which fell like flowers from his lips. As one learned professor remarked to me: 'No-one will ever know if Nandi peeked.'

The first human teacher in the tradition is Svetaketu Auddalaki, who must have lived between 1000 and 900 BC. His work was abbreviated by Babhravya of Panchala, whose latest date must be the fifth century BC. We know this because two of his seven scholiasts are mentioned by Kautilya, the chief minister of the Mauryan emperor Chandragupta (reigned *c.* 320–296 BC). None of the seven books of these scholars, each based on one of the divisions of Babhravya's text, have survived to modern times. The immense length of these works meant that the love teachings were in danger of collapsing, like a stranded whale, under their own weight, and so Vatsyayana composed *Kama Sutra* as a summary of all that was known about the subject.

Kama Sutra, like the *Arthashastra* of Kautilya, is composed in *sutra* style, perhaps because Vatsyayana wanted to elevate the art of love to a science. 'Prose is the touchstone of poets', so said the literati of the time, and Vatsyayana's prose is remarkable for its brevity and accuracy. 'A grammarian who can lose half a syllable from a line is as happy as though his wife had borne a son' – another saying from the ancient world. Brevity and the use of strong rhythms, of course, were necessary in an age which relied heavily on the oral transmission of texts. Like all *sutra* texts, *Kama Sutra* was designed to be a skeletal abstract of its subject, requiring extensive commentary. The most famous of the commentaries, the eleventh-century *Jayamangala* of Yashodhara, is nowadays printed alongside the text, which without it would be largely unintelligible.

Kama Sutra was a great success in its own time, eclipsing all previous works, and it has been recognized as a masterpiece in India ever since. In the sixteen centuries since its composition no imitator, and there have been many, has even remotely challenged its pre-eminence. The most famous of the medieval texts are the *Ratirahasya* of Pandit Kokkoka (better known as *Koka Shastra*, 'Koka's Treatise') and the *Ananga Ranga* of Kalyana Malla, composed in about the twelfth and sixteenth centuries respectively. Both texts are in verse; Kokkoka's the better, although Kalyana Malla is constantly referring to himself as the 'Prince of Poets'. Both follow *Kama Sutra* for much of its length, although adding a new classification of women and many sexual postures not found in Vatsyayana. They are strictly imitative works, however. It is astonishing to find Kokkoka retailing information given by Vatsyayana about the sexual proclivities of the women of Pataliputra, which had been lying in ruins for four centuries by the time he was writing, and Kalyana Malla describing the ideal bedroom in terms identical to those used by Vatsyayana some thirteen centuries earlier.

The later texts, and there are dozens, grow increasingly febrile. The inventiveness of their authors seems to have confined itself to describing ever more preposterous love postures. (Those which it may be even remotely possible to enjoy have been included in the present chapter on love positions.) None of them have Vatsyayana's freethinking spirit – he at least never hesitated to disagree with accepted authority – but follow one another slavishly.

The one exception I have found is a *Kamakalasara* of uncertain date, written in folksy *bhraj-bhasha*, which in its use of rhythm, assonance and imagery is reminiscent of the English ballad tradition. The *bhraj-bhasha* dialect is chiefly known for the mystical works of poets like Surdas and Kabir, so it is refreshing to find it expressing the robust sentiments of some seventeenth- or eighteenth-century village Vatsyayana. A fair translation of the opening lines might be (with apologies to the unknown author of *Sir Patrick Spens*):

> Oh, the king he sits in old Patna town,
> A-grovelling at Kali's shrine-
> And it's how may I father a bonny young prince
> To carry on my fathers' line-

The resultant instruction in the arts of love follows the usual pattern, but is far more entertaining.

The tradition continues to this day. Works in Sanskrit still appear, monotonously regurgitating classical and medieval ideas, and spicing them with a few new thoughts. Condemning masturbation is, for instance, one of the newer obsessions. The 1947 *Ratikelikutuhala* of Pandit Mathura Prasad is powerful on the subject, and the recent Hindi *Kokasaravaidyaka* of Narayanaprasad Mishra descends into outraged anecdote as one habitual masturbator, caught in the act, quotes a Sanskrit verse in defence of his persuasion.

The most modern works are those you may buy on almost any street corner in Bombay or Calcutta today. Shrink-wrapped in garish yellow cellophane, they are known as 'yellow books' and rejoice in titles like *Kok Shastra* and *Old Kam Sutra*. That they have nothing whatsoever in common with the texts they claim to represent is illustrated by the extraordinary statement in *Old Kam Sutra* that: 'A man should intercourse when his left nose blows.'

If *Kama Sutra's* reputation in India is now in the hands of the pavement booksellers, in the West it has rested far too long on the 1883 version of Sir Richard Burton and F. F. Arbuthnot. Burton, who though a brilliant orientalist was not a Sanskrit scholar, worked from an initial English draft made by four *pandits* who had collated various incomplete manuscripts, the corruptness of which may account for the more glaring errors in their work. In trying to infuse style into the *pandits'* broken English, Burton inevitably loses much of Vatsyayana's sublety. And his Victorian habit of concatenating upwards of twenty separate *sutras* into paragraphs sometimes two and a half pages long turns *Kama Sutra's* delicate observation into dry and often baffling reading. Against this one must set the fact that Burton was a pioneer, with no previous translation to guide or inform him, and that *Kama Sutra* formed only a tiny part of his research, of which *The Arabian Nights* was his greatest triumph, into the manners of the ancient East.

The only other English translation I have come across is by S. C. Upadhyaya, and this proved a useful work, breaking up the text *sutra* by *sutra*, quoting Yashodhara separately for the most part, accompanied by a great many indices and a scholarly essay on Indian erotic literature.

The most accurate translation, and the one which has helped me most, is the scholarly Hindi version of Devadutta Shastri in the Chaukamba edition of Vatsyayana's original text. My own work would have been virtually impossible without this translation, and I have also drawn extensively on Shastri's excellent commentary.

The aim of this translation is above all to restore Vatsyayana's ideas to life and to bring out their relevance for the modern reader. I also felt that the new version should in some way attempt to echo his terse, aphoristic prose *sutras*, written in the highly elliptical style for which Sanskrit, with its wealth of synonyms and its double-jointed syntax, was so perfect. In the end, I chose to compose in short five-line prose stanzas, hoping to recreate something of the mood of Vatsyayana, while trusting that this small discipline would not lead me too far from the original.

My method was to make an accurate translation of the original, *sutra* by *sutra*, adding notes from Yashodhara's commentary and uncovering what puns, ironies and purely prosodic effects I could, combining all this information in a loose prose draft and then expressing it, when I felt I had gauged Vatsyayana's intentions clearly, within the constraints of my chosen form. I should like, at this point, to express my gratitude to Professor S. A. Upadhyaya of Bharatiya Vidhya Bhavan, Bombay, who gave up several weeks of his valuable time to go through the Sanskrit text with me, clearing up various difficulties. Any major deviations from Vatsyayana are, however, entirely my own responsibility.

All translations of *Kama Sutra*, including this one, are necessarily paraphrases which, as Comfort points out, draw upon large chunks of Yashodhara's commentary. The nature of the *sutra* form renders a purely literal translation of no interest or value except to scholars. For instance, a literal rendering of the *sutra* in which Vatsyayana describes the *Vadavaka* technique (p. 60, '*Samputa* Group') would have to read: 'Like a mare cruelly gripping. That is the Mare, learned only by practice.' Perhaps if scholars, who have neglected the text for so long, feel the lack of a purely literal interpretation strongly enough, someone will publish an edition with Yashodhara translated separately. My own version is intended for the layman who does not necessarily know anything about India. It is therefore discursive and eclectic and does not pretend to be of academic interest.

Liberties I have taken include talking to the reader in the second person throughout, for instance changing 'the man should' to 'you should' and 'her husband' to 'your husband'. I have also, for the reason given above, expanded ideas, images and references that would have needed no explanation for ancient, or even modern, Indian readers, but which the Western audience might otherwise find mystifying or meaningless. I have omitted much that is of purely academic interest (especially from Book VI), abbreviated some chapters and simplified or restructured others where this seemed justified. Various source-books have provided me with material about everyday life in ancient India, but an astonishing number of gaps could be filled simply by observing life in modern India. *Paan* is still as popular and *paan-wallahs* as influential as ever they were in Vatsyayana's time. The same foods are still eaten, the identical cosmetics and incenses used; the same flowers perfume the night air; the same festivals are celebrated, and the eternal astrologer is still consulted before every wedding. It seems very important to me, a measure of the work's stature, that it is still a live text, still relevant today. Even the sections on courtesans and harem ladies could have been taken seriously until just over thirty years ago, when the princely states submerged their identities in the Indian republic.

I have added sections from the other major Indian works on love where they seemed to amplify *Kama Sutra*, for instance to demonstrate how the love positions flow in their almost musical sequences. The descriptions of these postures in the medieval texts are all too often obscure, however, or ambiguous. I have often had to guess what a poet meant before describing the posture as unequivocally as I could in modern English. This is, so far as I know, the first time that any attempt has been made to collate these texts, and the first time that several of them have been rendered into English. The descriptions of the Lotus Lady and the other three were known in Vatsyayana's time from the system of Gonikaputra, and became conventions in the poetry and drama of classical Sanskrit, as we see when Kalidasa describes Shakuntala as languishing in a fever of love, her burning limbs perfumed with the scent of crushed lotuses, and again in the descriptions of lovelorn Radha in Jayadeva's *Gita Govinda*.

The miniatures which accompany this translation, some of which were painted especially for erotic texts or to illustrate poems like the *Gita*

Govinda, are far more recent productions than *Kama Sutra* and the medieval texts yet, curiously, this does not affect their aptness. The temple sculpture of Khajuraho and Konarak was perhaps more directly influenced by Vatsyayana's work, but these temple-figures in their voluptuous abandonment seem almost austere, absorbed in a vision that we cannot share. The miniature paintings, like Vatsyayana, deal with love on a human scale. Their delightful details recreate so vividly for us what it must have been like to live in the courts where they were painted. And although in some cases the miniatures postdate *Kama Sutra* by as much as fifteen centuries, it is astonishing how little Indian life had changed in its basics over that time. How little, indeed, it has changed right up to the present day. Time and again, a miniature will remind me of some detail, cooking, or preparing a *paan*, of life in my grandparents' house. And my grandmother still hides her spices, onions and other vegetables in odd little corners of the house, just as the virtuous wife in *Kama Sutra* is enjoined to do.

The earliest surviving Indian paintings, which predate *Kama Sutra* by a couple of centuries, are to be seen on cave walls at Ajanta and Bagh. But Vatsyayana's reader, who is advised to keep drawing materials and brushes in his bedroom, would have painted on smooth stones, cloth or palm leaves, composing according to the rules laid down in *Vishnudhar-mottara Purana* and *Natyashastra*, both of which date from the second century AD. Holy sages were to be emaciated, with matted hair, their skin shining. Prostitutes were to be gaudily clad and heavily made-up. Gods were to have no hair besides eyebrows and eyelashes. Married women were to be elegant and moderately made-up, drawn proportionally smaller than their husbands. There was a whole language of posture, derived from the dance. It was said that without a knowledge of dancing, the rules of painting were impossible to understand. *Natyashastra*, the treatise on drama, gave colours to various moods. Red expressed anger, yellow the supernatural and the erotic sentiment was best conveyed by darkish colours. The inclusion of birds, flowers, musicians, bees and moonlight all helped heighten the erotic mood. These ancient treatises influenced painters well beyond their own era. Just as medieval and later poets still followed the rules of classical composition, so the painters of the Rajasthani and Pahari courts worked with the old texts in mind.

Large cities of Vatsyayana's time contained *chitrashalas* or art galleries, which generally stood at a cross-roads, or opposite a temple or royal palace, and which were lit by numerous windows and mirrors. The houses of wealthy citizens were decorated with murals. Courtesans had their bedroom walls covered with erotic paintings, early forerunners of some of the works reproduced here.

The earliest miniature in this book, painted in the reign of the Mughal emperor Akbar, dates from the sixteenth century when paper first came into general use. The arrival at the Mughal courts of painters from Persia and beyond had a powerful influence upon the older Hindu tradition. Jain and early Malwa art, under the Islamic influence, developed into Rajasthani court painting, with separate sub-styles flourishing at Udaipur, Jodhpur, Bundi, Kotah, Jaipur and elsewhere. The fusion of Hindu and Islamic influences can be seen again in the northern Punjab schools, which developed out of the simple, rather abstract Basohli style into the glories of Guler and Kangra painting. The Mughal influence was felt more directly in the Deccan, at the court of Golconda (later Hyderabad) and lasts until the nineteenth century in the increasingly feeble Oudh (Lucknow) school. From the early nineteenth century onwards European influence spread from Bengal into Lucknow and produced what is known as the Company style. The Lucknow dancing-girl on page 163 shows traces of what one might call subaltern-souvenir taste.

All miniatures were prepared using the same ancient techniques. The preliminary drawing was made with charcoal or pencils modelled from cowdung, powdered slag and water. The paper was then coated with zinc oxide and the final drawing made with the help of the faint outlines that showed through. Colour was applied with light strokes of a brush, made from the soft ear-hairs of bullocks and calves, or from the tail-hairs of cats, muskrats, squirrels and goats, which were fixed with shellac to pigeon or peacock quills. For painting tiny dots, for instance pearls, a round-tipped brush was used. Fine details required a brush with a single hair.

White pigment was obtained from burnt conch-shell or white earth, black from carbon, yellow from orpiment or the urine of a cow that had been fed exclusively on mango leaves for a few days. Red was obtained from red lead and vermillion from crude cinnabar mortared with sweetened water or lime juice. Blue came from lapiz lazuli, or more commonly from indigo which, with lac dye and carmine, was one of the principal vegetable colours. Gold and silver powder and red and black inks were also used. Colours were fixed with gum arabic or *dhau* gum and mixed according to very ancient and detailed formulae. Yellow with lampblack in proportions of two to one produces, for instance, the skin colour of the lower castes, while that of the upper castes is provided by equal amounts of yellow myrobalan dye, white and vermillion. Red ochre blended with conch-shell lime powder gives the exact shade of smoke. Colour was applied first to the foreground and background of the painting, and next to the bodies and clothes, when gold highlights were also added. The finishing touches were the pearls on pieces of jewelry, the reddening of hands, feet and lips and, finally, the completion of the eyes, which gave life to the figures.

Hindu painters loved to illustrate religious and epic themes. The legend of Radha and Krishna received particular attention. The Mughal court painters preferred portraiture, hunting scenes and recording royal occasions, and consequently these subjects are also common in Rajasthani painting. The attempt to define the moods of various *ragas* (Indian musical scales) and of the different *nayikas* or heroines (see pages 141 and 167 for examples of *vasakasajja* and *abhisarika nayikas* respectively) is common to all schools. Alongside all these, *tantra* and *yoga* art, designed for meditation, produced abstracts of pure form and colour which compare with the work of modern Western masters like Klee, Kandinsky and Rothko. The tradition, despite the sterile period that followed the imposition of Western taste on nineteenth-century painting, still continues today in folk art all over India.

A school of miniature painting still flourishes in Udaipur and at nearby Nathadwara and, while some of the painters seem to produce more eighteenth-century paintings than twentieth, a great many more are beginning to paint the world they see around them. One hopes that they, as well as the *gharanas* of classical musicians and the various schools of dance, will help to keep the classical tradition alive in India, preserving it from a too rigid formalism and allowing it to comment on the present. Which, of course, is also the aim of this book.

Bombay/London 1979–80

BOOK I
MEDITATIONS

ON THE LOVE TEACHINGS

Dharma is the root
from which Artha grows
and Kama flowers;
every word in this Kama Sutra celebrates
Dharma in Artha in Kama[1].

So too its author salutes
the masters
whose thought and teachings enlighten
these sacred subjects:
in their work this work is rooted.

When Prajapati[2] created men and women,
he sang them
one hundred thousand songs
to teach them how to consecrate their lives
with *Dharma, Artha* and *Kama.*

Manu, our forefather, kept the *Dharma* teachings;
Artha was Brihaspati's province,
and Nandi, horned watcher at Lord Shiva's door,
spoke aloud one thousand lovely chapters
about the art of *Kama.*

An aeon passed before those flowers,
fallen from Nandi's lips,
were gathered up and threaded by Svetaketu,
son of Uddalaka Aruni,
into a *Kama Sutra* of five hundred chapters.

And Svetaketu was an ancient name
when Babhravya of Panchala[3]
distilled the wisdom
to a work of one hundred and fifty chapters,
grouped under seven separate heads.

This was the famous *Babhravyakarika*[4],
divided in these seven sections:
Meditations, Lovemaking,
Courtship, Marriage, Other Men's Wives,
Courtesans and The Aphrodisiacs.

But Babhravya proved too scholarly
for Pataliputra's courtesans,
who finally tempted the old sage Dattaka
to lecture them for several months
on 'Courtesans', the sixth part of the work.

Babhravya's 'Meditations'
became Charayana's doctoral dissertation;
the arts of 'Lovemaking'
Suvarnanabha's thesis, and 'Courtship' became
the whole life's work of Ghotakamukha.

Gonardiya wrote volumes on 'Marriage',
while Gonikaputra won a sophist's reputation
for his work on 'Other Men's Wives'.
Nothing much was left for Kuchumara
but the spells and potions of 'The Aphrodisiacs'.

Babhravya's master work
was torn in pieces by these seven authors
and, since Dattaka and his friends
talked only of their pet obsessions,
the central *yoga*[5] of the science was lost.

Babhravya can't now be restored:
his work's too long, his language too archaic
for the modern taste;
so Vatsyayana has composed this slender abstract –
our entire knowledge of love.

---

1. Instead of the customary exordium to a deity, Vatsyayana pays his respects to the three great aims of Hindu life. These crucial terms have no English equivalents, but *Dharma*, loosely, is spiritual and moral duty, *Artha* is intellectual and material wealth, and *Kama* is all sensual pleasures. See Introduction for a fuller discussion.

2. Brahma as the Creator. See Glossary for all proper names, place names and titles of texts.

3, 4. See Glossary

5. When the science is taught in separate sections, the central thread, the binding *yoga*, or yoke, is lost.

The god Shiva in his aspect as destroyer. The animal skins mark him as an ascetic and the five heads symbolize divinity and omniscience. His third eye is usually closed as it burns up whatever it gazes upon. Shiva once burned the love-god Kama to ashes for disturbing his meditations. He is attended by his servant and doorkeeper, the white bull Nandi. The subdued, delicate palette is typical of the rather ethereal paintings of the Kangra school. *Kangra, c. 1830 (detail)*

ON THE TRIPLE QUEST

Man, who lives at most one hundred years,
should seek *Dharma*, *Artha* and *Kama*
in different ways at different times of life,
the sages say,
to avoid chasing three ways at once.

In boyhood he should fix his mind on *Artha*,
in youth touch *Kama* with his senses,
and in old age let *Dharma* still the mind and body,
to spare him
further visits to this world[1].

But swords and sickness make life uncertain
so Vatsya says seek *Dharma*, *Artha* and *Kama*
whenever you may,
however you can, with this proviso only:
you must be celibate in your student years.

Dharma is lived
outwardly by obeying the word of the *Vedas*[2],
by, for instance, sacrificing and forsaking meat;
inwardly by practising the *yoga* texts[3]
and being in the presence of great teachers.

Artha is education, houses, land, grain, cattle,
gold, clothes, jewels, friends, the arts,
gaining, husbanding and multiplying wealth.
Farmers and rich merchants can teach it,
but its greatest experts are the king's taxmen.

Kama is the delight of body, mind and soul
in exquisite sensation:
awaken eyes, nose, tongue, ears, skin,
and between sense and sensed
the essence of *Kama* will flower.

It is the breath of lip on lip,
the caress of breasts, hips, buttocks, thighs
in the beautiful embrace
from which a child is born:
learn it from *Kama Sutra* and the world.

In general, since *Dharma* is the root,
you should set
Dharma before *Artha*, *Artha* before *Kama*;
but a wise king seeks *Artha* for his country's sake,
a courtesan uses *Kama* for her own good.

The Need for Kama Teachings

Fallacy
According to some teachers
there is a need for texts on *Dharma* and *Artha*
as they are difficult to grasp,
but since even jungle animals make love together
there's no need to go writing books on *Kama*.

Reply
Kama can be terrifying to those
with deeply-rooted fears
or inhibitions.
The love teachings free men and women
to accept each other's emotions without fear.

Kama is powerful.
It can wreck marriages and reputations,
but the couple who study its arts
become lovers of such skill
that their love can never be destroyed.

Kama is blind in animals,
mere rutting while the females are in heat,
but men and women
who know its *yoga*
embrace infinity in their lovemaking.

The Need to Practise Dharma

Fallacy
The atheists, who have exchanged the *Vedas*
for Charvaka's ironies[4],
are fond of saying that the fruits of sacrifice,
meant to sustain us in the future life,
may very well prove inedible.

Better a pigeon today than tomorrow's peacock,
a copper safely in one's pocket
than a promise of gold: who is such a fool
that he'll exchange wealth he can touch
for wealth whose very existence is in doubt?

---

1. The four stages (*ashrams*) of a Hindu's life are celibate studenthood (*brahmacharya*) until the age, roughly, of twenty-five; marriage (*grihasta*) until the age of fifty; retirement from public life (*vanaprastha*) up to the age of seventy-five, and the existence of a wandering ascetic (*sannyasin*) thereafter until death. Because Vatsyayana's commentator Yashodhara omits the third stage, it is commonly held in India that *Kama Sutra* advises an active sexual life until the age of seventy or more.

2. The four great religious books of the early Aryans. See Glossary for *Vedas* and separately under *Rig Veda* and *Atharva Veda*.

3. Patanjali's *Yoga Sutra*, the earliest extant Indian *yoga* teaching, was written in about the first century AD and would have been known to Vatsyayana.

4. See Glossary

A scene from *Ramayana,* the second of the great Hindu epics. *Brahmin* priests intone
sacred passages from the *Vedas* and make ceremonial offerings of rice to the holy
fire, from which the god Agni rises to accept the sacrifice. These rituals are still
performed in India today. This *Ramayana* set was probably painted for Rana Jagat
Singh of Mewar, who built the famous marble lake palaces of Udaipur.
Udaipur, c. 1649 (detail)

Reply
Knowledge of the *Vedas* kills doubt.
Their rites of exorcism and invocation are seen,
by all, to work; their formulae
have harnessed the sun, moon, stars and planets
to work for the benefit of mankind.

Society is founded upon the four classes
and four ways of life[5],
all of which have their origin in the *Vedas*;
and is it really so foolish
to sow seed-corn in hope of future crops?

The Need to Practise Artha

Fallacy
The fatalists believe it's quite pointless
to exhaust oneself seeking wealth –
most men stay poor, however hard they sweat,
while others grow rich without working –
their philosophy stops at *'que sera sera'*.

They say that profit, loss, defeat, success,
pain and pleasure
are spots on Destiny's ivory dice;
Destiny set Bali on Indra's throne,
Destiny toppled him and alone can restore him.

Reply
Realize that Destiny is not lying in wait,
it's with you here and now;
it's not the road you walk, it is the walking[6].
Whether friend or enemy, it always
answers to your name – for you are Destiny.

Control the Self, and Destiny
acts within you, wills within your will,
uncoils the universe within.
But even Destiny needs a nudge –
leave fatalists to blame their fate on Fate.

The Need to Practise Kama

Fallacy
Some people practise *Dharma* and *Artha*,
saying *Kama* is to be ignored
because ascetics,
whose way of life is sanctioned by the *Vedas*,
have turned their backs on pleasure.

They say that men who hunt for pleasures
find sensuality and sin;
they mix with scum
who lead them into crime,
and end despised, spat out by society.

Men enslaved by sexual passion
ruin their families with themselves.
King Dandakya of the Bhojas
raped a *brahmin's* daughter
and died with his nation under a rain of dust.

Indra, king of the gods, debauched Ahalya;
Kichaka insulted Draupadi;
the warlord Ravana kidnapped Sita[7],
and all, despite their strength and fame,
were utterly destroyed.

Reply
This is great nonsense, for sex
is as vital to the body as food and drink
and should be sought as innocently.
Vatsyayana says *Kama*
is the flower and fruit of *Dharma* and *Artha*.

Fear of sex should not prevent its practise;
no-one, after all, stops cooking food
because a beggar may come to the door,
or sowing barley
because wild deer may nibble it in the fields.

The Triple Quest
Artha, Kama, Dharma:
the man or woman who knows all three
and acts with body, mind and soul
always here and now,
is happy through this world and in the next.

Kama, Dharma, Artha:
know two of them, or even one,
if you can't know all three,
but never practise
any one at the other pair's expense.

---

5. The four classes are the priest (*brahmin*), the warrior
(*kshatriya*), the merchant (*vaishya*) and the labourer (*shudra*).

6. This interpretation of these two very difficult *sutras*
(Chaukamba I 2: 30–31) owes a great deal to the *Aitareya
Brahmana* (VII:13–14) quoted in Shastri's Hindi commentary,
and to conversations with various teachers.

7. See Glossary

The dense, eerie jungles of Kotah, in southern Rajasthan, have always dominated the paintings of that region. Here a Kotah prince, possibly Durjan Sal, hunts wild boar. The courtier with the sword may be the same man who once despatched a tiger with a single swordstroke. The nightmarish, almost psychedelic jungles of early Kotah painting have given way to a gentler forest in which monkeys and herds of deer play. It was on just such an expedition that Dandakya, twenty-five centuries earlier and three hundred miles to the south, met his doom. *Kotah, c.1810? (detail)*

ON THE ARTS AND SCIENCES

Young men should add to their study
of the sciences and arts
prescribed in the *Dharma* and *Artha* texts,
the *Kama Sutra*
with all its related arts and sciences.

A virgin living in her father's house
should know the theory
of *Kama Sutra* by her wedding night.
With her husband's approval
she should grow more expert after marriage.

Some greybeards have said
that as women and every kind of science
are mutually incompatible,
it's nothing but a colossal waste of time
to try to teach them *Kama Sutra*.

But how absurd, says Vatsyayana,
to forbid the study of this science to women,
and yet encourage them to practise it!
The practice of a science is gravely limited
by ignorance of its laws.

Sacrificial priests, devoid of grammar,
parrot invocations and are forced
to interpret the sacred texts by guesswork.
People ignorant of astrology
can scarcely benefit from observing the stars.

However skilfully some horsemen, charioteers
and elephant-riders weave
their powerful mounts through battles,
breaking-in a *sarpa*[1] or a *danava*[2]
would be a fight they could not hope to win.

The people of remote provinces
obey the kingdom's laws
because they know the king has a large army
with lightly-sheathed weapons,
but this doesn't make a nation of barristers.

Anyway, it's common knowledge
that there are princesses and ladies-in-waiting,
to say nothing of courtesans,
whose expertise in dancing and the arts of love
makes even *Kama Sutra* seem redundant.

A young girl should study *Kama Sutra*
with an older woman
in whom she can have complete confidence,
but practise by herself
the sixty-four Babhravyite love techniques[3].

Her guide should be a childhood friend
experienced in love,
a young aunt or old family servant,
a well-travelled ascetic
or, best of all, a favourite elder sister.

There are, besides *Kama Sutra*,
sixty-four important arts and sciences
(quite distinct from
Babhravya's sixty-four)
which are essential to her education:

Singing.
Performing on musical instruments.
Dancing.
Painting on walls, palm leaves and smooth stones[4].
Cutting letters into *bhurja* leaves[5].

Creating *mandalas* in flowers and rice[6].
Decorating walls and floors with flowers.
Colouring the body, hair, nails, teeth and clothes.
Making mosaics.
Arranging couches, beds, cushions and carpets.

Playing tunes on glass bowls filled with water.
Swimming and water games.
Meditation using *mantra* and *yantra yogas*[7].
Threading garlands, necklaces and rosaries.
Making flower head-dresses for weddings.

Dressing and wearing jewels with style.
Making conch and ivory bangles and earrings.
Blending perfumes.
Inlaying with semi-precious stones.
Magic tricks and illusions.

Preparing aphrodisiacs and herbal charms.
Sleight of hand.
Cookery of several schools.
Mixing sherbets, fruit punches and cocktails.
Sewing and embroidery.

---

1. The name given to a horse of irascible nature in the *Ashvashastra* (Horse Lore) of Nakula.

2. A rogue elephant, instructions for the taming of which are found in the *Matangalila* (Elephant Sport) of Nilakantha.

3. These are discussed in greater detail at the beginning of Book II, Embraces.

4. From references in Kalidasa's *Meghaduta* it is clear that portraits were often painted on small smooth stones. The glorious cave murals of Ajanta were begun in Vatsyayana's period and are the earliest surviving works of what may have been a much older tradition.

5. Birch leaves. The Jaipur poet Vyakulji has an old pair, one with animals cut into it, the other with birds, which when held up together combine to form a love-letter in *devanagari* script.

6. Circular designs on the floor, within which family deities are worshipped. It can also mean a sorcerer's charmed circle.

7. *Mantras* are religious formulae, often a god's name (eg *Hare Rama Hare Krishna*), which are meant to be repeated constantly. *Mantra yoga* is one of the Transcendental Meditation techniques taught by Maharishi Mahesh Yogi. *Yantras* are symbols for meditation, usually painted in simple shapes and strong colours.

The Mughal emperor Akbar listens to his court musician
Tansen playing *sitar* and singing. The accompanist plays a
tampura or drone. Tansen was a musician of such consummate
skill that he was said to have charmed deer out of the forest and
rain from clear skies. The *raga* of rain which he created and
which is called, after him, *Mia ka Malhar* is still a favourite with
Indian singers. The painting, with its fine brushwork, slightly
elongated figures and almost meditative calm, shows the
influence of the court of Aurangzeb, Akbar's great-grandson.
Kishangarh, late seventeenth century

Weaving birds and flowers in silks and wools.
Expertise in classical *raga* and *tala*[8].
Solving riddles.
The *antyakshari* game of capping verses[9].
Composing tonguetwisters.

Chanting from sacred texts.
Quoting aptly from epics and dramas.
Improvising poetry.
Basketwork with cane and reeds.
Fashioning gold and silver sexual aids[10].

Woodcarving and carpentry.
Architecture and the science of building.
Assaying gems and precious metals.
Ore refining and alloying.
Mining, cutting and colouring gems.

Horticulture and plant medicine.
Training fighting rams, cocks and quails.
Teaching parrots and mynahs to speak.
The art of scalp and body massage.
Code-breaking and a knowledge of ciphers.

Inventing a private language.
Fluency in dialects and foreign languages.
Making flower chariots.
Reading omens and auguries.
Constructing sprinklers and other machines[11].

Memory training.
Flawless repetition of once-heard verses.
Composing a lyric from random letters
or by arranging petals.
Knowledge of dictionaries and thesauri.

Facility with poetic metres.
Disguise and the arts of Muladeva[12].
The art of draping cloth
and making cotton appear like fine silk.
Gambling.

Dice and chess[13].
Child psychology and children's games.
Etiquette and bearing.
War, weapons, armies, tactics, statecraft.
Yoga and gymnastics.

A girl who is modest, beautiful
and skilled in these arts
can win fame as a courtesan:
all society from kings and scholars down
falls over itself to honour her.

A lady widowed in a foreign land
can use these arts to make a handsome living.
A princess expert in these arts
is always royal favourite,
even in a harem of one thousand queens.

---

8. Respectively, the melodic and rhythmic components of Indian classical music. The science of music which, in Aryan India, originated in the heptatonic chants of the *Sama Veda* was considerably modified by the pre-Aryan pentatonic system and had, before Vatsyayana's time, been codified in Bharata's *Natyashastra*, a seminal work which dealt with music, drama and the dance, all of which, together with *yoga* and the love teachings, are said to have originated from the god Shiva.

9. One player recites a line of poetry, the last consonant or vowel of which becomes the starting point for the next player's line (eg: Shall I compare thee to a summer's day?/ A drowsy numbness pains my sense, as though of hemlock I had drunk/ Come keen Iambicks with your Badgers' feet, etc).

10. The types and uses of these are discussed in Book VII.

11. Kalidasa describes a *variyantra* (water machine) which may have been a whirling spray powered by water pressure (*Malavikagnimitra* II 12). In the palace at Udaipur there is a fountain cart which used to be wheeled along at the head of processions and was worked by a crank.

12. Sorcery and sleight of hand. See Glossary for Muladeva.

13. *Chaturanga* (Four Corps), the earliest forerunner of chess, had evolved from a dice game played on a board or cloth of sixty-four squares. In Vatsyayana's time each player would command one or two of the four armies on the board, each army consisting of a king, elephant, horse, chariot or ship, and four foot-soldiers. Moves were controlled by throws of a die. The game was learned in the sixth century by the Persians, who called it *Shatranj*, and it spread to Europe after the Crusades.

The gymnasts, wrestlers and archers of a Deccan court practise their sports. In
ancient times gymnastics and yoga were closely related, while boxing and wrestling
were the preserve of low-caste professional pugilists. Gladiators fought at the third
century BC court of Chandragupta Maurya. This painting was possibly painted at
the court of Asaf Jah I, whose descendents became the Nizams of Hyderabad.
Hyderabad, early eighteenth century

ON SOCIETY LIFE

Once your education is complete,
use what money you have,
whether acquired by gift, warfare, trade or labour[1],
to buy into a decent neighbourhood
and take your place in society.

Enclosed in a leafy garden by a river,
build a house with a courtyard,
kitchen, bathroom, stores and work-rooms,
a pretty *zenana* for your ladies[2]
and an airy master-bedroom.

Your bedroom should be perfumed,
and furnished with a soft, silk-canopied bed
whose clean white sheets
and plump bolsters
are strewn with freshly-picked flowers.

Set a couch nearby for lovemaking;
at its head a table
with collyrium, beeswax candles, flower-strings,
paan[3] for perfuming the breath,
and strips of citron bark.

Near this couch should be a cuspidor,
your jewel case, a *vina*[4]
suspended from an elephant's tusk,
brushes, drawing sticks, some favourite books,
and fresh garlands of yellow amaranth.

Complete the room with a circular rug,
and ivory boards for dice and chess.
Just outside have cages
of parrots and songbirds,
and a workshop for carving and other hobbies.

In your garden build a love-seat
shaded by jasmine creepers,
and hang a swing beneath the branches of trees
that will release each spring
monsoons of fragrant blossom.

After relieving yourself each morning
you should clean your teeth with twigs of *neem*[5],
rub a little sandal-oil
into your forehead and temples,
and brush collyrium on your eyelids and lashes.

Perfume your hair in incense smoke,
garland yourself with amaranth or jasmine,
redden your lips with *lac*, chew *paan*,
and check your appearance in a mirror of silver
before going out to meet your friends.

Take a bath daily in running water,
have a massage every second day,
use soap each third day,
have your face shaved every fourth day,
depilate your body every fifth or tenth day.

Eat a light breakfast at eleven
and dine more heartily at sunset.
(Charayana insists that dinner be at eight.)
After breakfast, spend an hour
training your mynahs and parrots to speak.

In the early afternoon be seen
at cock or ram fights,
and while away the lazy hour before siesta
sharpening your wits
on jesters and buffoons.

Go with your friends each evening,
richly dressed and jewelled,
to a tavern or house of pleasure
where the talk is art, philosophy or politics,
or the singers are particularly fine.

Later, with that delicate music
following on the night,
walk home with one or two close friends
and light the incense for the hour
when your lover and her friends arrive.

Send someone to fetch her if she's late,
or go yourself,
but greet her warmly when she finally appears,
and entertain her friends
with wine and amusing conversation.

If a sudden shower has smudged her eyes
help her to repaint them,
and if her skirt is even slightly damp
insist that it's your duty
to take it off and towel her dry yourself.

The Festival of Sarasvati
As a citizen it is your duty
to help organize religious celebrations
and assist, with your friends,
at the fortnightly and monthly drama festivals
staged in the temple of Sarasvati[6].

---

1. He is referring to the occupations of the four classes. The *brahmins*, or priestly caste, lived on gifts and donations.

2. A women's sanctum, where men were not admitted.

3. Crushed nuts and spices wrapped in a *betel* leaf.

4. A long-necked Indian lute. The *sitar* has largely replaced it in northern India, but it is still the dominant stringed instrument in the south.

5. *Azadirachta indica* The bitter twigs are sold in small bundles for use as disposable toothbrushes.

6. See Glossary

A lady, holding her skirt out of the mud, braves a rainstorm to meet her lover. If he has read his *Kama Sutra*, he will follow Vatsyayana's cunning suggestion and offer to towel her dry. This outstandingly beautiful miniature, with its brilliant colours and charming rainstorm, is a fine example of the early work done at Basohli, a town perched like an eagle's eyrie in the foothills of the Himalayas. The man's costume shows Mughal influence and probably reflects the fashion of the reign of Raja Kripal Pal (1678–94), who first established an atelier at his court. The stark, almost primitive Basohli style that developed is possibly a fusion of Mughal and Jain influences. *Basohli, late seventeenth century*

On the opening day, the temple actors
should perform their plays.
An exceptionally sensitive performance
may be encored on the second day,
when the actors should also be thanked and paid.

During these festivals do everything you can
to help the priests of Sarasvati
(in an emergency, you may be asked
to play a role yourself),
and always pay your share of the expenses.

You should also be a generous host
to actors and gentlefolk
who have travelled a long way to the festival:
introduce them to your circle
and offer them the hospitality of your home.

These guidelines hold good
for celebrating festivals and feasts
at the temples of Shiva,
Krishna, Ganesh, Kama, Laxmi,
the Yakshas and all other goddesses and gods[7].

Literary Evenings
Delightful soirées may be held,
either at your place or at the house
of an eminent courtesan,
for friends and others of your age and rank
who share your interests.

The conversation should be distinguished
by its wit and grace, and should touch
upon poetry, the arts, law, science and politics.
Quiz each other on the latest books,
and devise impromptu poetry competitions.

The winners of these contests
(who will more often than not be courtesans)
should receive amusing prizes,
and visiting artists, gentlefolk and scholars
should also somehow be honoured.

Parties
When it's your turn to give a party,
decorate your house
with strings of richly-scented flowers,
set lights all through the garden
and invite your friends and favourite courtesans.

Serve only the finest wines:
madhu of a blend in which the wild honey
does not overpower the grape,
liquorice-perfumed *maireya,*
fragrant mango *sura* and wood-apple *asava.*

Serve foods that complement the wines:
light snacks in spicy sauces,
green vegetable salads,
fresh fruit, baked breads, chutneys and relishes,
sweet pickles and salted nuts.

Picnics
Choose for your picnic a green garden
by a river that falls
pool by pool through woods down a hillside,
or near a forest lake
about an hour's ride from your home.

Wearing fine clothes, set out on horseback
as dawn is breaking,
accompanied by friends and young courtesans,
followed by singers,
musicians, and servants carrying food and wine.

Spend a pleasant day placing bets
on rams and fighting-cocks,
listening to the music and the singers,
dancing, dicing,
playing chess and other games of skill.

Go swimming with the ladies
if it's hot enough
and crocodiles or weeds present no danger.
Bind flowers in your hair
and start for home as dusk draws down the sky.

Religious Festivals
On the Night of the Yakshas[8]
your house should be outlined in fire,
with tiny earthen lamps
set close along each wall and window-ledge
and bonfires in the garden.

On full moon night in October
make the fire-sacrifice
to Indra, Pashupati and the Asvins[9].
Float their banners from your rooftop
and strew the five flowers on your threshold.

On the fifth night of the Spring Moon,
put aside your winter clothes,
and light the fires for Shiva, Sarasvati and Kama[10].
Wear red filmy garments and red flowers,
and mark their effigies with fresh red powder.

---

7. See Glossary

---

8. Burton mistranslated *yaksha-ratri* (Night of the Yakshas) as *aksha-ratri* (Dice Night) and was thus led astray with what follows, which is a list of religious festivals. *Yaksha-ratri* is cognate with modern *diwali*, the festival of lights. See Glossary for Yakshas.

9, 10. See Glossary

This delightful painting, from an illustrated manuscript of *Madhumalati*, the story of a love affair between a king and the lady Malati, shows the king picnicking with Malati and her women on the shore of Ramasarovara Lake. It is not impossible that the painter drew his details from *Kama Sutra*, as he even shows a cockfight. The crude, angular drawing, and use of brilliant primary colours like lacquer red, saffron yellow and lapiz lazuli show the influence of the old Jain tradition. The manuscript records that it was made in the village of Nai, some six miles from Udaipur, which may explain the contrast with the Udaipur court style. *Udaipur, dated 1749*

Join with your family and friends
in observing each festival's ancient customs.
During the festival of Kama,
go out into the forest
to pick young mango flowers for your hair.

At the harvest, ride down to the fields
to roast ripe wheat and barley.
When summer heat begins to dry the lakes,
wade out to gather
the delicious tender stems of the lotus.

When the forest is in bud
go picnicking among the myriad greens,
and keep the *holi* season[11]
by celebrating in the streets
with syringes of parrot-coloured dyes.

After nine nights of the autumn moon,
let Ravana burn,
and bring out old puppets, richly dressed
in old Panchala costume,
to re-enact the glories of *Ramayana*[12].

At spring equinox play hide and seek
under the moonlit
blaze of Flame-of-the-Forest trees.
Form laughing armies on warm May nights
to pelt each other with yellow *kadamba* blossom[13].

Gentlemen travelling far from home
should, if they can,
celebrate these festivals by themselves.
Ladies whose lovers are away
should celebrate them with their maids.

Friends and Associates
You will have several kinds of friends:
first those with whom you played
as a child in the dusty lanes of your village,
next the children of your nurse,
and people who are endebted to your family.

Then there are the friends
you met at school and university,
friends who share your temperament and tastes,
and those with whom you share
closely guarded secrets or confidences.

Give to these friends what you ask of them:
loyalty to their families,
pleasant and congenial companionship,
support in difficult times
and whole-hearted affection at all times.

Never insult a friend by lying to him,
always encourage his ambition,
and delight in his success.
Don't tempt him to vices or addictions,
and never break your word or his trust.

Make friends with *pithamardas*[14],
wandering teachers of the arts and sciences
who, destitute save for their red robes,
wooden stools and bars of soap,
tutor young men and courtesans for a living.

Cultivate *vitas*, gentlemen who,
having squandered their fortunes on courtesans,
use their exquisite manners
and boundless store of sexual profundities
to earn both honour and their livings.

Vidushakas are essential allies,
fellows who live entirely by their wits;
jesters, gossips, counsellors,
whose skill at making delicate connections
also makes them indispensible.

Other Obligations
If your home is in the countryside
it is your duty to school the villagers
of your caste in etiquette,
to help them out of trouble and to share
the benefits of your city education.

Never patronize a villager by speaking
only his dialect, nor confuse him
by using high-flown literary Sanskrit.
Careful blending of the two
ensures both comprehension and goodwill[15].

Take care to avoid bad company,
secret or anarchic sects
that advocate practices which are degrading
and which harm others:
a wise man seeks his pleasure innocently.

---

11. The spring festival in honour of Kama, the god of love.

12. See Glossary for *Ramayana*, the second of the great Hindu epics. I have followed Shastri's interpretation of *Panchalakrida* as signifying the 'Panchala doll game'. The festival chimes with modern *Dassera*, when excerpts from the *Ramayana* are chanted, actors re-enact important scenes and huge wicker effigies of Ravana are burned before crowds of enthusiastic worshippers.

13. *Antheocephalus indicus* The tree, according to legend, only blossoms during the storms that presage the monsoon.

14. *Pithamardas*, together with *vitas* and *vidushakas*, were stock characters in Indian drama whose roles approximate, perhaps, to the minor comic characters in Shakespearean tragedy. In life they were parasites on wealthy households.

15. Sanskrit (literally 'perfected') was the language of the educated few. The rustic masses spoke various dialects, or *prakrits*. Modern Hindi is descended from the *prakrit* spoken over much of northern India in Vatsyayana's time. Yashodhara, Vatsyayana's eleventh-century commentator, must have spoken early medieval Hindi, because Hindi expressions often creep into his *Jayamangala* glosses.

The late spring festival is celebrated by the ladies of the Bundi palace while the Maharao and his favourite watch from the roof. In anticipation of the storms to come, the *frangipani* trees are flowering. The pond filled with lotuses, birds and fish is a typical Bundi motif, as are the flowering trees. The women wear traditional Rajasthani skirts in the gaudy hand-printed cottons which have recently become popular in the West. *Bundi, c.1770*

ON LOVERS

Choose virgins of your own caste
to be your wives and bear your children;
only sons of such unions
are considered, by society and the *shastras*[1],
respectable and your legal heirs.

You may go, purely for sexual pleasure,
to courtesans, widows, divorcees,
and women of lower castes than your own;
it's neither commended nor condemned
as the question of marriage does not arise.

The *shastras* forbid you even to dream
of making love to a woman of a higher caste
or to any married woman.
(Manu says wives who sleep with low-born men
should be torn apart by dogs[2].)

But Gonikaputra allows the seduction even
of a high-caste married woman,
listing instances where ethics may be suspended
because she is already corrupt
or she can help you to achieve some vital goal.

'Lovely Malati, though she's married
and *brahmin* to boot,
is such a tireless nymphomaniac
that there's surely no more sin
in bedding her than flirting with a courtesan[3].'

'Kallolini's certainly no virgin
and has in any case ditched her husband
for that actor Natyasvami;
seducing her can only make
her poor husband a cuckold once-removed.'

'No-one could accuse Vikarala of beauty,
but her influential husband
is far too friendly with my rival Bhattadayada;
the beauty in seducing her
is the wedge she'll drive between those two.'

'Sundarasena is too dangerous a man
for his enmity to be ignored;
the lesser danger lies in wooing his wife
who, being a bit of a *rakshasa*[4],
will give him hell till he leaves me in peace.'

'Old Kusukarna, who can ruin my enemies
and raise my friends to power,
is firmly under his young wife Manjari's thumb;
I'd be a fool not to grasp
the golden opportunity between her thighs.'

'Haralata's hatred of her drunken husband
makes her easy to seduce,
and if one night he stumbles from a whore's arms
into a pair of tiger-claws,
his wealth will be inherited by the tiger.'

'I am good-looking, but destitute
and unable to support myself;
Madhuraksi is ugly but very wealthy,
and her husband is abroad;
I shall find a fortune in his empty bed.'

'Kesara is so drunk with lust
that she's threatened, unless I sleep with her,
to drum my indiscretions all round town!
She has added that she'll ruin me with lies
impossible to refute with honour.'

'She also swears to turn her husband
into a relentless enemy
and set him plotting with my rivals;
she's going to say I forced her
and encourage him to seduce one of my wives!'

'For a long time I have suspected
that Lalita's husband
has been selling military secrets to the Shakas[5];
by using her to expose him
I'll place the king deeply in my debt.'

'Anangadevi will have to be seduced.
Only she can help me win
that rich, disdainful beauty, Kamasena,
her closest friend,
who has driven me crazy with desire.'

'Out of love for me Chitralata
would sleep with Matta,
who is a man I fear very greatly,
giving me the chance
to betray him to her husband's sword.'

---

1. A general term for all religious and scientific texts.

2. *Manu Smriti* (VIII: 371), composed about AD 200. I have included this comment to demonstrate how serious a crime adultery with a low-caste man was considered, and to underscore the outrageousness of Gonikaputra's excuses.

3. In the original this list of excuses is so baldly presented as to make them sound, at times, utterly ridiculous. Dramatizing each situation at least makes it less incredible. The names are filched from Damodara Gupta's *Kuttani Mata*, a ninth-century poem comprising the advice of an old prostitute to a young one.

4. One of the types of women described in the exhaustive and rather ludicrous classification of Bharata's *Natyashastra*. The name, and this lady's temperament, derive from a class of hideous, bloodthirsty demons.

5. Enemies of the Gupta emperors. See Glossary.

A heavily be-jewelled lady of the Jaipur court. She wears
rubies, pearls, emeralds and what might be a ring of carved
jade. Could she be the concubine Ras Kafur, described by her
contemporary, the historian Tod, as 'a common prostitute, the
favourite of the day', to whom Raja Jagat Singh is said to have
given half his wealth? The rose-pink city of Jaipur is still famous
for its jewelry, enamelwork and stone and marble carving.
Jaipur, c.1790

Vatsyayana says these dangerous seductions
are only ever justified
when there is a pure, honourable motive
and then as desperate last resorts,
never because you simply desire the woman.

Some scholars hold that housekeepers,
shaven-headed nuns,
virgin daughters of servants and courtesans
and single girls of good family
are four more classes of women you may enjoy.

But as most young men, says Vatsyayana,
would much rather bed a girl than classify her,
let's be done with hair-splitting
or we'll soon be classifying eunuchs
(so far unclassified) as yet more sorts of women.

Avoid sexual contact with any woman who
is leprous, insane,
disowned by her family or caste,
cannot keep secrets
or is promiscuous or withered by age.

Avoid women whose skins are ivory white,
or black as charcoal,
or whose bodies smell disgusting.
Avoid blood-relations,
childhood companions and beggar-women.

Never touch the wife of a relative,
friend, high-priest or king;
ignore Babhravya's commonly quoted dictum
that these women may be enjoyed
if they have slept with five or more lovers.

From the Medieval Texts

The Padmini (Lotus Lady)[6]

Her face is as lovely
as the full moon on a clear night,
her rounded limbs are soft as walnut flowers,
fragrant as the lotus,
as fair as petals of *frangipani*[7].

Her eyes are sloes
with sharply pointed corners dipped in red,
wide as a startled fawn's.
Her nose is a little sesamum flower,
her lips trembling sprays of scarlet *bandhujiva*[8].

Her heavy breasts
are firm as ripened pomegranates,
like jars of beaten gold;
high they ride,
twin bosses on the brow of Kama's elephant.

Her slender waist
is girdled with three creases[9],
her *yoni* is like a newly-opened lotus bud[10],
her love-water scented
as delicately as crushed lotus stems.

She walks with wide hips swaying
gracefully as a swan
and has the black swan's low, sweet voice.
She dresses in pure white
and never forgets her duty to the gods.

Modest and intelligent,
highly skilled in the sixty-four arts,
a fine singer and musician,
she eats sparingly and sleeps lightly:
such is the lotus lady.

The Chitrini (Lady of Dance)[11]

Her curls are swarms of black bees
framing a pretty face
from which peep a pair of bright restless eyes
and a small pair of lips
that pout like a pair of ripe red *bimba* gourds[12].

Her neck is shaped
like an auspicious three-ringed conch;
her heavy breasts, jutting
above a tiny waist,
bend her slender body like a bow.

She walks with swaying hips,
lascivious as an elephant in *must*[13],
her full-globed buttocks
rolling on slim round thighs
that taper to ankles as delicate as a crow's.

Her *yoni* is a gentle hill
clad lightly in fine wispy hair,
yielding within,
quickly wet with love-juices
that smell powerfully of wild honey.

_____

has velvety-white petals, touched sometimes with pink, and a deep butter-yellow heart. The flowers are very fragrant.

8. *Ixora coccinea* Medieval poets thought it by far the choicest metaphor for a beautiful woman's lips.

9. The three creases, or *trivalli*, are both auspicious and a sign of great beauty.

10. The female sexual organs.

11. Literally 'picture lady', the second of the medieval types.

12. A small ridged cucumber, the modern Indian *karela*.

13. The drunken behaviour of an elephant in heat.

_____

6. The *padmini*, or lotus woman, is a stock in trade of all the medieval texts, which describe her as the ideal of womanly beauty. This description is an amalgam of those in *Ratirahasya*, *Ananga Ranga* and *Ratimanjari*, which influenced countless poets. Some details are also taken from *Gita Govinda*, *Ritusamhara* and *Kuttani Mata*. Most of the great Indian heroines, including Sita, Draupadi and Shakuntala, are supposed to have been *padminis*.

7. *Plumeria rubra forma acuminata santapau* The temple tree. It

In this delicate painting from the Kangra valley, in the northern Punjab, a lonely maiden yearns for her absent lover and envies the happiness of the birds that bill and coo at her feet. The ancient *Natyashastra* classified heroines or *nayikas* into eight groups, according to mood. Technically, this painting shows a *padmini* lady in the *utkanthita* mood. The lyrical line and dreamy air is typical of the Kangra school, which developed under Raja Sansar Chand, in whose reign this painting was executed. *Kangra, c.1790*

She prefers a cuddle to making love
and needs to be aroused with lips and fingers.
Her voice is like the peacock's,
but in her confusion
she will stammer like a moon-crazed *chakora*[14].

Neither very short nor very tall,
she is a skilled dancer, singer and musician,
good also at the visual arts
and at making clothes and ornaments;
she has a taste for very slightly sweet things.

The Shankhini (Conch Lady)[15]

Although not petite,
she is really much smaller than she looks;
her slender body
and smooth, boyish limbs
give an unfair impression of height.

Her small breasts are firm,
her waist slim though not curvaceous;
she moves swiftly,
swinging long legs and arms
in a rangy stride like a young man's.

She has a demure pointed face,
with slanting almond eyes
whose pupils are brown flecked tiger gold;
she is self-possessed
and goes unveiled, meeting people's eyes.

Her *yoni* is deep
and thatched about with thick curly hair.
It is hard to make her wet;
her love-fluid is salt
and smells like slightly sour molasses.

She is always eager for sex
and very passionate,
losing control of her limbs during lovemaking,
flailing with her fists,
pinching, scratching and nipping her lover.

She is often sulky or spiteful,
and loves red clothes and scarlet flowers
which match her hot temper;
in a rage her natural clear contralto
sounds like the splendid snorting of a wild ass.

The Hastini (Elephant Woman)[16]

She is plump all over, in every limb
from her short neck
carried on stooping shoulders,
to her arms, breasts,
belly, hips, buttocks, *yoni*, thighs and feet[17].

She moves slowly, as though wounded,
her gait unlovely, flat-footed,
curling up her toes with every step,
her reddish-brown hair
swinging forlornly in a tail behind.

Her lovers are ashamed of her
and quickly abandon her,
so she is both shameless and abandoned
in her efforts to win new lovers,
her big lips always greedy for kisses.

Her *yoni* and her whole body
smell of elephant-nard.
Her *yoni* is a cavern between her thighs,
flooded with love-fluid,
lost in a thick black hairy jungle.

She comes so slowly to orgasm
that only a master of love can satisfy her,
yanking back her hair,
his hand vigorously churning her *yoni*,
for she likes violent lovemaking.

She eats hot, spicy and sour foods
in enormous quantity.
Her speech is stuttering and shy.
She is bad-tempered but also
loyal, affectionate and very kind.

---

14. The Indian red-legged partridge, which has a staccato call and which, by poetic convention, is said to feed on moonbeams.

15. The third of the medieval female types.

16. The fourth of the medieval female types. The poets were almost universally scathing about her. I have followed the tone of *Ratimanjari*, the most charitable of them.

---

17. In texts of *Ananga Ranga*, the word *gaurangi* (fair-limbed) is surely a copyist's error for *gaurvangi* (heavy-limbed). Burton compounds this with the absurdity that: 'her skin, if fair, is of a dead white'.

In all medieval love texts we encounter the extraordinary idea that Kama, the god of love, not only dwells in women's bodies but migrates from place to place according to the phases of the moon. This late, rather crude painting from Udaipur is almost unique in having been made especially to illustrate this absurd idea. The artist has carefully labelled, on the left, the parts of the body and, on the right, given instructions to the husband: 'Kiss the cheek', and so on. *Udaipur, nineteenth century*

BOOK II
LOVEMAKING

COMPATIBILITY

Although the holy texts divide
men into four classes,
Kama acknowledges only three,
determining caste strictly by penis length:
the hare, the bull, the horse[1].

Kama likewise classes a woman
as doe, mare or elephant[2],
according solely to her *yoni's* depth.
Doe with hare, mare with bull,
elephant with horse: these are equal partnerships.

With couples whose dimensions
do not nicely correspond,
there are six degrees of mis-match:
elephant with hare or bull,
mare with hare or horse, doe with bull or horse.

Equal couplings are best:
extreme conjunctions (elephant with hare,
doe with horse) seldom satisfy.
With the remaining pairs, success depends
largely on temperament and skill.

There are three sexual temperaments:
passionate, moderate and cold.
A man with a cold nature feels little desire;
his semen does not spurt vigorously;
he tries to avoid his lover's nails and teeth.

Passionate men can't hide their lust,
while moderate men can keep it in control.
Each type has his female counterpart,
adding to the physical couplings
nine possible relationships of temperament.

Finally, the degree of a lover's skill
is determined by how far
he or she can prolong the pleasure of making love.
Lovers may be expert, adequate or unskilled,
giving nine further permutations.

Fallacy
A controversy about the need for skill
centres on the woman's role.
Auddalaki[3] says that women, unlike men,
get no physical release from lovemaking,
but joy from satisfying their lovers.

Expertise in kissing and caressing,
in varying the postures to prolong lovemaking,
certainly enhances a man's pleasure,
but women do not need it
as their pleasure is of a quite different kind[4].

No man or woman will ever know
exactly what the other feels while making love;
no words will ever describe it,
but man's pleasure is ended by orgasm
while woman's pleasure never comes to an end.

Reply
Why then is it a fact
that women adore the man who can stay an hour
and despise the one who is gone
in two quick thrusts?
Doesn't this prove they too want orgasms?

Fallacy
It would be unnatural, say the sceptics,
for a woman to experience
intense emotional pleasure during lovemaking
and yet not wish it to continue.
They even quote Auddalaki's verse to this effect:

'In swyvynge man the luste
Of blisful woman doth abate,
Yet ne kisse, love-drurye, ne thruste
Of phallos doth her passioun sate,
But knowliche of hire herte mate.'

Babhravya adds that unlike a man,
whose semen-spurt comes at the end of pleasure,
a woman's seed flows from the start,
flooding every limb with joy,
thus she has no need for long lovemaking.

Reply
This is Auddalaki in disguise.
If she feels such pleasure from the start,
why is she at first so still,
her body only gradually yielding to the passion
which in the end shakes her so violently?

Could it be that a woman's passion
is like a potter's wheel, or a child's top,
spinning at first slowly
and gathering speed until at last it blurs
in the mindless beauty of release?

1, 2. The dimensions given in the medieval texts are: the hare and doe, six fingerbreadths; the bull and mare, nine fingerbreadths; and the horse and elephant, twelve fingerbreadths. There is no connection between this elephant woman and the *hastini* of the medieval texts.

3. See Glossary

4. This rather boorish view seems also to have been common in ancient Rome. Lucretius, in *De Rerum Natura*, says: 'Certainly wives have no need of lascivious movements. A woman makes conception more difficult by offering a mock resistance and accepting Venus with a wriggling body . . . These tricks are employed by prostitutes so that they may not conceive so often and, at the same time, may make intercourse more attractive to men. But obviously our wives can have no use for them.'

Here a perfectly balanced pair of lovers hold a posture that has elements both of *Kaurma* and the *Yugmapada* of *Ratirahasya* (see p. 66), and which may be an intermediate stage between the two. Achieving balance and with it stillness was especially important in *tantric* sexual rites. The painting is carefully organized to emphasize the theme of passion under control. *Udaipur, late eighteenth century*

Babhravya has himself written:
'His spasm is his pleasure's end,
Whilst her fierce ardour knows no cease,
For in love's battle both must spend
And blend their seed ere she finds peace.'

Since man and woman are both human,
both engrossed in the same act,
why on earth should their pleasure differ?
Vatsyayana concludes
that women have an orgasm just as men do.

Fallacy

But man and woman are not the same!
A man is to a woman
what the quern-stone is to the quern:
they are made differently,
have opposing natures and separate roles to play.

It is not in the least ridiculous
to suppose that, because a man and a woman
differ from one another
both in body and in temperament,
they experience pleasure in quite different ways.

Reply

It is obvious even to Vatsyayana
that man and woman are shaped differently.
He accepts also that by custom
men dominate and women are dominated –
and of course their lovemaking reflects this.

Man's nature has always been to crow
'I am making love!',
while she coos 'This man is making love with me!';
but the pleasure, when it comes,
cannot tell which is the woman, which the man.

When rams crash heads in the arena,
when wood-apples collide,
when two giant wrestlers clash in combat,
the shock runs equally through both,
and so it is when a man makes love to a woman.

Don't now object that rams are rams,
wrestlers wrestlers, but men not women.
Man and woman are one nerve, one blood,
one muscle, bone, sinew, soul:
there is no difference, none, beneath the skin.

Linga and *shakti*[5] are shaped to one another,
for how else could new life be born?
Desire yokes a man and a woman in one love,
one passionate union,
to create a child from one shared pleasure-shock.

Vatsyayana says that every woman
should know the joy of orgasm.
Every man should learn love's skills –
the kiss, caress, *asanas*[6], teeth and nail games –
and seek his lover's pleasure before his own.

Since no two lovers will ever quite
match each other in size, temperament and skill,
there can be no rules to govern lovemaking.
Only experience can tell you
which techniques will satisfy which lovers.

The wise know also that physical pleasure
is not the sole end of lovemaking.
It can be like music, stirring the emotions,
quickening the senses, dissolving
thought into rhythm, until only rhythm exists.

On and on it flows as hearts thud faster,
limbs tremble in the beat
of drums that double pace and double again,
till music itself breaks
into one long holy note of silence.

Love has many *yogas*:
the touching of two bodies; the locking of groins;
the drawing apart in separation;
the quieting of the violent breath;
the still release from body and mind.

People of intelligence and sensitivity
will find these remarks
sufficient to elucidate this delicate subject[7].
For those who need further enlightenment,
the arts of love are now described in detail.

---

5. The penis and vulva. The symbols of Shiva and Parvati were
worshipped conjoined in the form of standing stones set in
lipped basins.

6. Postures. The term is common to the love texts, *hatha-yoga*
and the dance, all of which originated from Shiva.

7. See Introduction for a discussion of these *sutras*.

'The quieting of the violent breath.' Erotic paintings are far less common in Basohli art than, for instance, in that of the Rajasthan courts, but this picture, with its startling shapes and colours, makes brilliant use of Basohli conventions. The posture is *Vyomapada* from *Ananga Ranga*, but the artist has shown the man using his fingers to control his wife's breath, and this is almost certainly a depiction of *Nadi Sodhana Pranayama* (Nerve-cleansing Breath-control) as adapted for *tantric* practice.
Basohli, early eighteenth century

45

EMBRACES

The ancient writers on erotics teach
that an expert lover should know
the sixty-four lovemaking techniques
as well as the sixty-four arts
and sciences discussed in an earlier chapter.

Some say these sixty-four techniques
were first defined by Babhravya,
in ten chapters which he wrote in pious imitation
of the *Rig Veda's* ten *mandalas*[1],
divided into their sixty-four sets of hymns.

Babhravya gives eight techniques
to each of the following eight subjects:
embraces, kisses, nailmarks,
lovebites, postures,
lovecries, role reversal and oral sex.

But some of Babhravya's subjects
have more and some fewer than eight techniques.
He discusses loveblows, pelvic movements
and the temple postures[2],
yet finds no room for them in his 'sixty-four'.

This famous phrase, says Vatsyayana,
is like 'the tree of seven leaves',
'the rice of five colours': we use these terms
knowing that neither is the tree seven-leaved
nor the offering five-coloured.

The Embraces
Slightly acquainted men and women
can make their feelings known to one another
by using the Touch or the Stab.
The Caress and the Squeeze
are for lovers who know each other's desires.

When she approaches you,
acting as though she doesn't know you're there
and, as she passes, lets her hand or body
brush lightly against yours,
it is the embrace called the Touch.

When a woman, seeing you nearby, advances
exclaiming that she's dropped something
and stoops to pick it up
so that her hard breasts pierce your body,
(you are to caress them slyly) it is the Stab.

When you walk together at night
in a crowded *bazaar*
or stroll down a quiet country lane,
your bodies nestling into one another's curves,
their delicious frisson is the Caress.

When you press her up against a pillar
or back into a doorway,
shocking the breath from her body,
and each of you now lets your hands explore
the other's limbs, it is the Squeeze.

Babhravya gives four further embraces
for more experienced lovers.
The Creeper and the Tree are done standing,
the Sesame & Rice and the Milk & Water
often melt without warning into lovemaking.

When she twines her arms around your neck,
like a creeper on a *sal* tree[3],
lifting her face for your kiss,
then pulls back a little, breathing hard,
anxiously scanning your face, it is the Creeper.

When she places her feet on yours
and climbs your body as though she were a vine,
grasps your waist with her thighs,
grabs your shoulder, uttering little moans,
and bends your head for kisses, it is the Tree.

When you lie facing one another
with thighs interlaced, her breasts pressed
to you, hands seeking new places
to caress, pulling heads together for kisses,
the embrace is like the mixing of Sesame & Rice.

When she winds her legs about your waist
and presses her loins to yours
in an embrace so violent that your bodies,
oblivious to pain, seem almost
to penetrate one another, it is the Milk & Water.

These are Babhravya's eight embraces.
Suvarnanabha gives four more
in which different parts of the body are aroused
for lovemaking: the embraces
of the thighs, groin, breasts and forehead.

---

1. Song-cycles. See Glossary for *Rig Veda*.

2. *Chitrarata* could be translated 'picture positions', but since these postures are the ones most commonly depicted on temple walls at, for instance, Khajuraho and Konarak, it seems to me at least possible that this implies how they got their name. The more extraordinary and exotic postures were also favourites with medieval painters and engravers of palm-leaf manuscripts and there is no reason to suppose that this was not also the case in Vatsyayana's time.

3. *Shorea robusta* A large gregarious tree, typical of northern and central Indian jungles. The aromatic gum that oozes from the trunk is an aphrodisiac.

The lovers are in an embrace which could be said to be a sort of reversed Creeper. Above all the artist has tried to express the tenderness they feel for one another, and the painting is in the ethereal, lyrical style which originated in the hill states of the Punjab and the Himalayan foothills. The label *Pahari* (Mountain School) indicates simply that we do not know for certain at which court this rather late work was painted. *Pahari, nineteenth century*

When, as you lie in each other's arms,
she traps one of your thighs
and squeezes it powerfully between her own,
her muscles soaking up the pleasure,
it is known to experts as the Thigh Embrace.

When she raises beautiful thighs
and pulls your groin against her mound of Venus,
drives her nails into you, nips, sucks kisses
from your lips, her hair tumbling
loosely about her face, it is the Groin Embrace.

When she climbs over you,
letting your chest take the full weight
of her heavy breasts,
tracing circles with them on your body,
it is called by experts the Breast Embrace.

Each of these three embraces may also
be initiated by the man.
When you place foreheads together, eye to eye,
nose to nose, lip to lip, caressing
one another's faces, it is the Forehead Embrace.

Some teachers class massage with embraces
since it gives physical pleasure,
but Vatsyayana says that as the aim of massage
is to remove weariness, not stir desire,
it cannot be included with the arts of lovemaking.

Even those who ask, hear or speak
about these embraces
will, if they are properly described, find
desire stirring in their bodies.
Those who use them will have keener pleasure.

There are many very lovely caresses
which have never been mentioned in the texts.
You should discover them with your lover
and use them whenever you can
if you find they sharpen both pleasure and desire.

The texts on love can only be useful
while desire is still,
but once that potter's wheel begins to turn,
my dears, throw down even *Kama Sutra*,
for then there is no law, no rules, no science.

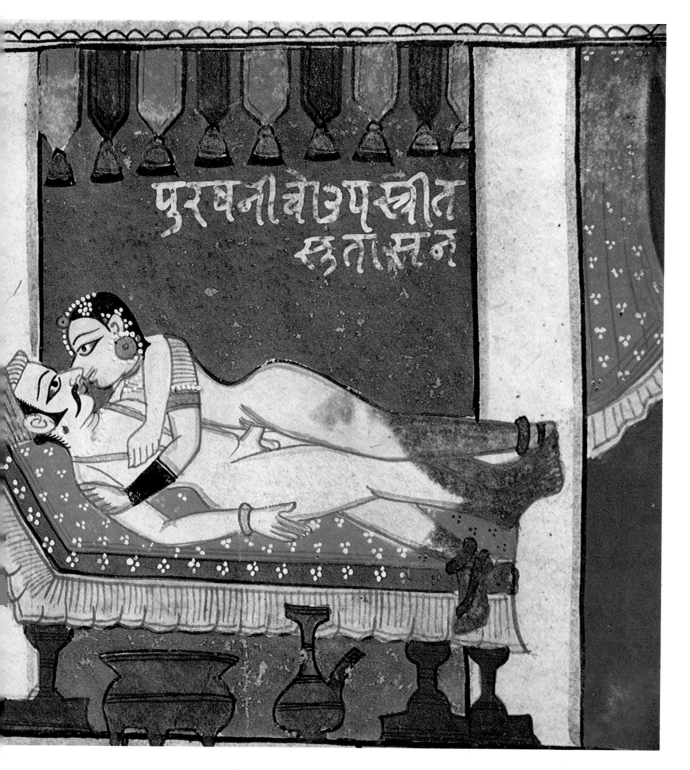

A close and passionate embrace, says Vatsyayana, can turn
without warning into lovemaking, and these lovers are twined
in a knot reminiscent of what *Kama Sutra* calls the Sesame & Rice
embrace. The attendant holding a torch looks discreetly away.
Making love in front of an audience of servants does not seem
to bother these haughty Rajput nobles and their ladies. This
miniature, with its curious earthy palette, was one of a set
probably painted at the minor court of Sirohi. *Sirohi, eighteenth
century*

KISSES

Kissing, marking with the nails
and making lovebites
should, some say, always precede lovemaking,
while the loveblows and lovecries
should be used only to hasten your lover's orgasm.

But Vatsyayana says once passion
is aroused there is little time for protocol.
You may do whatever you like
whenever you please, since Kama
respects no conventions and can't be regimented.

The first time you sleep with a girl
don't overdo the kissing, nails and teeth –
one thing at a time is best.
But as her confidence increases use every trick
in this book to fuel her desire.

The Kisses
Place your kisses on her brow,
her curls, eyes, cheeks and lips,
her neck and breasts,
and send your tongue on pilgrimage
to all the holy places of her sweet mouth.

A man from Lat[1] would also kiss
the monkey tufts under her arms, her navel,
thighs and secret lips.
This peculiarly violent display of passion
reflects his nationality – it's not for everyone.

Three kisses are especially charming
when given by young girls.
These are the Almost-not-a-kiss,
the Trembling Kiss
and the delightful First-touch-of-her-tongue.

The first is when your nervous new bride,
on being pestered for a kiss,
reluctantly allows herself to be embraced
and accepts the homage of your lips,
keeping hers, however, clamped fiercely together.

When she has gained confidence
she may permit her lips to part a shade.
If you then nibble her lower lip
and feel it trembling as pleasure surprises fear,
you've won through to the second kiss.

One day her eyes will close;
you'll feel her hands creep up to cover your eyes
and a tongue shyly enquiring
if it may proceed to more adventurous things –
this third kiss ends her apprenticeship.

The love texts have four more kisses.
Lips meeting squarely make a Straight Kiss
and at an angle a Slanted Kiss.
You tilt her chin to steal a Lifted Kiss,
and any of these, if fierce, is a Crushing Kiss.

Some writers call it Pressing Wine
when, grasping her chin,
you pinch her mouth to an 'O'
and, making sure your teeth don't hurt her,
kiss her hungrily and hard.

Kissing Games
Lay wagers on who, using lips only,
can first capture the other's lower lip.
If she loses she should cry,
wagging her hand at you and saying it's unfair,
you've cheated and she wants another chance.

When you quite rightly refuse,
she should bite your nose and sulk
till you agree to her unceasing demands.
And if you win again
she should create an even greater fuss than before.

If she can get you off guard
she should quickly seize your lip in her teeth,
claiming through her laughter
to have won a famous victory,
and threatening to bite if you try to escape.

She must proclaim victory shrilly,
taunting you with skeins of the choicest abuse,
using every nuance of expression
her beautiful eyes and eyebrows can command,
to dare you to risk your pride in another contest.

You should invent other kissing games
and contests of nails and teeth,
whoever loses behaving in the manner prescribed.
These games greatly arouse desire
and prolong the pleasure of lovemaking for hours.

---

1. See Glossary

Between the thirteenth century AD, when the sculptors of Konarak covered the Sun
Temple in dozens of rapturously kissing couples, and 1978, when Zeenat Aman
horrified Indian film critics by passionately kissing Shashi Kapoor in *Satyam Shivam
Sundaram*, the kiss seems to have disappeared from Indian public life. The man in
this painting may be kissing his lover as they make love, moving into the
Paravrittaka posture (see p. 66) and if so he is probably using the gentle kiss *Mridu*.
Mewar, early eighteenth century?

If, as she kisses your upper lip,
you suck her lower lip, it is the High Kiss.
If both her lips are caught by yours
(she can return this kiss
only if you're clean-shaven), it is the Clasp.

If during this kiss your tongues,
while exploring each other's teeth and palates,
should meet in fierce jousting,
it is known as the Tourney of Tongues.
Other battles may be fought with lips and teeth.

Four kisses use lips, teeth and tongue together.
Sama[2] is given on the breasts,
in the sensitive crooks of knee and elbow
and where the thighs join the body:
nibble delicately and tickle with your tongue.

Pidita[3] is especially for the cheeks,
breasts, belly, hips and buttocks,
where your teeth may sink deep into her flesh
without hurting her at all
while lips and tongue massage her vigorously.

Anchita[4] is a tongue kiss
that trails the curves underneath her breasts,
probes her navel-well and lingers
at her secret lotus,
stirring desire but proposing no relief.

Mridu[5] is using your lips to soothe
the tingling in her back, hips, breasts, arms
and the insides of her thighs
after your nails have raked lightly across,
causing tiny body-hairs to rise and stand on end.

When she gazes at your sleeping face
and kisses your mouth
to wake you and kindle your desire,
her long, intensely passionate kiss is called
Ragadipa, Love-flickering-into-flame.

If you ignore her because you're absorbed
in music, painting or an argument,
or because you've quarrelled with her,
and she surprises you with a very loving kiss,
it will be *Chalita*, the Kiss of Deflection.

If you come home late to find her sleeping
and kiss her tenderly,
it is *Pratibodha*, the Kiss That Awakens.
She, for her part, should pretend to be sleeping
when she hears your voice at the door.

If you wish to express love for a lady
to whom you dare not speak
and kiss her reflection in a lake or a mirror,
or her shadow on a wall,
it is *Chhaya-Chumbana*, the Kiss of Shadows.

If, for the same reason, you kiss a child,
leaf-portrait or marble figurine,
so that your feelings are quite unmistakable
to the lady who is watching,
it is *Samkranta*, the Kiss by Metaphor.

If your lover is near you at the theatre
during an engrossing play,
or sitting not far off at a caste-gathering,
and you convey kisses by fingertip
to her toes or fingers, it is the Covert Kiss.

A masseuse will show her desire
by dropping her head
and kissing you swiftly on your thighs or toes
in a way that fools spectators
into thinking she has fainted from exhaustion.

The man who accepts his lady's kisses
but gives none in return
is about as desirable as a cold stone pillar.
To kindle her passion you must
match her kiss for kiss, caress for caress.

---

2. Even, flat

3. Pressed, squeezed

4. Curving or curling

5. Delicate, tender

An extravagant way to steal what Vatsyayana calls a Lifted kiss. The painting bears
an extraordinary resemblance to a sculpted group on the Vishvanath temple at
Khajuraho, in which the lovers' long leaf-shaped eyes seem to be closed in
anticipation of the meeting of their lips. Perhaps the painter had travelled to
Khajuraho and seen the temples. *Mewar, late eighteenth century*

NAILMARKS AND LOVEBITES

Once passion is stirring,
lovers should bring their nails into play.
The effect is electrifying:
under a lady's nails even the most diffident lover
feels his body slowly charge with desire.

Nail-play is especially exciting
the first time lovers go to bed together;
on the nights before and after a long separation;
after a blazing row,
and when she's had a little too much to drink.

Good nails are long and shapely,
even, silky to the touch,
clean, shiny, not torn or broken;
their faint scorings should be
the same healthy pink as the body of the nail.

Passionate types allow the nails
of their left hands to grow long and sharp.
Some file them into two or three points,
like a saw-blade,
others file them to crescents and parrot-beaks.

The love texts say you should mark
only your lover's armpits, breasts,
throat, back, thighs and groin.
But, as Suvarnanabha remarks, during lovemaking
no-one bothers to remember these things.

The Nailmarks
Eight techniques should be mastered:
Ripping Silk, the Half Moon,
Circle, Furrow and the Tiger's Claw,
the Peacock's Foot,
Leap of a Hare and the Petal of the Blue Lotus.

Draw your sharp fingernails
across her cheeks, breasts and lower lip
so lightly that no mark is left,
but, at the touch, her skin crawls in pleasure,
and you hear a sound like silk being ripped.

Use this tantalizing caress
when she begs you to massage her body or scalp,
commands you to scratch her back
or prick a nasty blister, and whenever
you choose to make her helpless with desire.

The Half Moon is a slender crescent
made with one nail on the throat and breasts.
A pair of crescents printed deeply
into the belly, hips, buttocks or groin
(like marks of parenthesis) forms a Circle.

The Furrow is a small red streak
ploughed through her skin by a sharp fingernail
almost anywhere on the body.
If curved it is a Tiger's Claw,
and is usually made on the breasts and neck.

When her nipple is caught
between five nails driving sharply together
in a sunburst of delicate red rays,
it is the famous Peacock's Foot –
difficult to make and prized highly by women.

If she shamelessly begs you
to make the Peacock's Foot upon her breast
and you, with five nails only,
score first one breast and then the other,
it is the virtuoso Leap of a Hare.

The Petal of the Blue Lotus
is made solely upon the breasts and waist
and is shaped as its name suggests.
To make this mark is considered a compliment
equivalent to giving a lady jewels.

It is most unchivalrous
to leave home on a long journey
without marking your wife's breasts and thighs
with at least three or four
small lines as mementoes of your love.

You should constantly invent new marks
to practise with your lover.
These could be shaped like birds, flowers,
waterpots, leaves, creepers –
but the possibilities are far too many to list.

Even to begin to catalogue
the infinity of potential shapes and techniques
(to say nothing of the bizarre marks
that passionate lovers will improvise)
is, the sages state, an utter waste of time.

In this luminous, very stylized painting, the royal lovers are shown in the posture of *Indranika* (see p. 58) named for Indrani, wife of the god Indra. On the man's cheek, there is a deep, angry mark, perhaps a Half Moon made by her nails, or the bruise of the Swollen lovebite, which was often made on the left cheek. The diaphanous *jama* of the prince is particularly finely handled. Compare the lady's face and jewelry to those of the girl on page 35. *Jaipur, late eighteenth century*

But Vatsyayana wishes to stress
the importance of variety in lovemaking.
Every fool knows variety-is-the-spice-of-life,
but only successful courtesans,
it seems, know it's also the essence of lovemaking.

Finally, never sink your nails
into another man's wife.
Content yourself with discreet crescents,
hidden where only she will find them,
to remind her of her secret trysts with you.

Lovebites

Every part of her body you would kiss,
excepting only her upper lip, tongue and eyes,
will also accept lovebites.
Even the places the Latas like to kiss
are suitable targets for an expert's teeth.

Good teeth are clean, shiny, even,
sharp, well-shaped and easily coloured by *paan*[1].
Chipped, dull, blunt, worn, dirty,
overlapping or protruding teeth
are best kept hidden; they're insults to a lover.

Eight famous lovebites need practice:
the Secret and Swollen bites,
the Dot and the Line of Dots,
the Coral and the Necklace of Corals,
the Stormcloud and the Wild Boar.

When you bite her lower lip,
reddening it but leaving no mark, it is the Secret.
If you bite until the lip bruises,
it is the Swollen (the swelling comes later),
which is often also made on the left cheek.

When you nip her skin so cleanly
that the bruise is no bigger than a sesame seed,
you have made a Dot; whole Lines of Dots
will look beautiful in the soft skin
of her neck, breasts and the hollows of her thighs.

The broken red curve of Coral
is made by biting only with the upper incisors.
Starting from her breasts or thighs,
Necklaces of Coral can be made to twist
in branching loops about her body.

The Stormcloud is a circle of marks
which should be gently printed on her breast.
A circle of deep, angry marks
bruised violet in the centre is the Wild Boar.
It is only enjoyed by very passionate people.

When nail and tooth marks are printed
upon *bhurja*[2] leaves or the blue lotus flowers
that girls wear behind their ears,
they act as amorous invitations,
and should be composed as carefully as love letters.

If a man ignores his lover's cries
that his nails and teeth are hurting her,
she should retaliate in kind,
but returning Tiger's Claws for Furrows,
driving off his Stormcloud with a Wild Boar.

In her passion a woman should grasp
her lover's hair, grip his lip
like the rim of a cup in her teeth, and drink
till lust intoxicates her and she bites
wildly, piercing his body in a hundred places.

When, next morning, he proudly shows
his friends the bruises
her nails and teeth have made upon his body,
she should stare at him poker-faced,
and only start to laugh once her back is turned.

In reply she may scold him angrily,
pointing with a grimace to her own bruises.
If they cherish one another
and twit each other affectionately,
their love will not fade in a hundred years.

1. See p. 28, note 3
2. Birch leaves. See p. 24, note 5

In ancient India it was considered so abnormal for a man to adopt a submissive role that the *purushayita*, or female-superior postures, discussed by Vatsyayana in the chapter on role reversal, were thought rather daring and consequently were rare delights. The creases that run from either side of her nose are deeply drawn, a characteristic that sometimes appears, although more delicately, in Guler painting.
Pahari, Sikh School, nineteenth century

LOVE POSITIONS

If your lover's smaller than you are,
choose love positions
which spread her thighs widely apart.
If she's a little too generous,
use those which draw them tightly together.

If she dwarfs you utterly,
pleasure her with a phallus of gold or silver.
But if the pair of you are nicely matched,
you may celebrate every posture known
in this beautiful *yoga* of two bodies.

Lying-down Positions

Utphullaka Group – Kama Sutra
The deer woman finds most pleasure
in the opened postures of the *Utphullaka* group:
Utphallaka (The Flower in Bloom),
Vijrimbhitaka (The Widely Yawning)
and *Indranika*, the posture of the goddess Indrani.

In *Utphallaka* she uses a bolster
to raise her hips high,
and spreads her thighs as widely as she can.
Enter her very gently
or you may injure her and hurt yourself too.

In *Vijrimbhitaka* her thighs are spread
and her legs stretched high,
while her hips remain firmly on the bed.
This greatly widens her *yoni*,
but tilts it downward, so enter her carefully.

Indrani draws up both knees
until they nuzzle the curves of her breasts;
her feet find her lover's armpits.
Small girls love this posture,
but becoming a goddess takes a lot of practice.

Utphullaka Group – Medieval Texts[1]
She cups and lifts her buttocks with her palms,
spreads wide her thighs,
and digs in her heels beside her hips,
while you caress her breasts:
this is *Utphallaka* (The Flower in Bloom).

(*Ratirahasya*)

Grasping the ankles
of the round-hipped woman, whose buttocks
are like two ripe gourds,
raise her beautiful thighs
and spread the thigh-joints widely.

Full of desire, saying sweet words,
approach her with your body stiff as a pole
and drive straight forward
to pierce her lotus and join your limbs:
experts call it *Madandhvaja* (The Flag of Cupid).

(*Panchasayaka*)

Catch hold of her two feet,
raising them till they press upon her breasts
and her legs form a rough circle.
Clasp her neck and make love to her:
this is *Ratisundara* (Aphrodite's Delight).

(*Smaradipika*)

Lift the lady's feet until her soles
lie perfectly parallel,
one to each side of her slender throat,
cup her breasts and enjoy her:
this technique is *Uthkanta* (Throat-high).

(*Ratimanjari*)

Your lovely wife, lying on the bed,
grasps her own feet
and draws them up until they reach her hair;
you catch her breasts and make love:
this is *Vyomapada* (Sky-foot).

(*Ananga Ranga*)

Clasping her own knees, your wife,
lying on the bed,
straightens her legs to lift her feet high
while you squeeze her breasts together:
this is *Vyomapada* (Sky-foot).

(*Panchasayaka*)

The round-thighed woman on the bed
grasps her ankles and raises high her lotus feet;
you strike her to the root, kissing
and slapping open-palmed between her breasts:
this is *Markata* (the Monkey).

(*Srngararasaprabandhadipika*)

She lies flat on her back,
you sit between her parted knees, raise them,
hook her feet over your thighs,
catch hold of her breasts, and enjoy her:
this is *Manmathpriya* (Dear to Cupid).

(*Smaradipika*)

Sit between your wife's thighs,
place your hands on the bed near her waist
and rotate your hips as you make love:
this is *Smarachakra* (Love's Wheel),
a great favourite with passionate women.

(*Ananga Ranga*)

---

1. See Glossary for the various medieval texts quoted in this chapter.

A prince or nobleman of Kotah makes love with his wife in the *Manmathpriya* posture. If she were to lift her feet to his shoulders the posture would change to *Jrimbhitaka*, from which a further sequence could be developed. The lady's loose hair, which indicates passion, is finely painted. Sometimes single-haired brushes were used to put in these minute details. Note the well-stocked box of *paans* beside the bed. *Kotah, c.1760*

She lies upon the bed of love
with arms and legs outflung like a starfish;
you fall upon her body, flattening
her two breasts and pressing them together:
this is *Ratimarga* (Love's Highway).
(*Srngararasaprabandhadipika*)

Samputa Group – Kama Sutra
If your penis is too small for a woman,
the *Samputa* group of postures should be used:
Samputa (the Jewel Case),
Pidita (the Squeeze), *Veshtita* (the Entwined)
and *Vadavaka* (the Mare's Trick).

In *Samputa* your legs lie along hers
caressing their whole length from toes to thighs.
Your lover may be below you,
or you may both lie on your sides,
in which case she should always be to your left.

In *Pidita* the lovers' thighs
are interlaced and squeeze each other in rhythm.
In *Veshtita* she crosses her thighs
or rolls each one inward,
thus greatly strengthening her *yoni's* grip.

When, like a mare cruelly gripping
a stallion, your lover
traps and milks your penis with her vagina,
it is *Vadavaka* (the Mare's Trick),
which can only be perfected with long practice.

When she uses it, a woman
should cease to kiss or caress her lover
and simply hold the lock.
Courtesans are adept at *Vadavaka*,
and it's a speciality with ladies from Andhra.

Samputa Group – Medieval Texts
When lovers, with legs stretched rigid
and feet caressing feet,
make love according to their hearts' desire,
tantra scholars call it *Samapada* (Equal Feet)
and agree it is a way to ecstasy.
(*Ratikallolini*)

Stiff as a pole in the bed's centre,
she lies making love,
cooing and warbling like a woodpigeon,
the jewel of her clitoris well-polished:
this is *Mausala* (the Pestle).
(*Srngararasaprabandhadipika*)

When she lies on her back
with her two thighs pressed tightly together
and you make love to her,
keeping your thighs outside hers,
it is *Gramya* (the Rustic).
(*Ratirahasya*)

If, encircling and trapping
her thighs with yours,
you grip so hard that she cries out in pain,
it is *Ratipasha* (Love's Noose),
a device most charming to the ladies.
(*Smaradipika*)

Her limbs, entwined in yours
like tendrils of fragrant jasmine creeper,
draw taut and slowly relax
in the gentle rhythm of *linga* and *yoni*:
this is *Lataveshta* (the Clinging Creeper).
(*Ratimanjari/Ananga Ranga*)

She draws her limbs together,
clasping her knees tightly to her breasts,
her *yoni*, like an opening bud,
offered up for pleasure:
this is known to experts as *Mukula* (the Bud).
(*Srngararasaprabandhadipika*)

When she draws up her knees
and you clamp yours about her raised thighs,
trapping them in a tight knot
while riding saddle upon her buttocks
and kissing her, it is *Shankha* (the Conch).
(*Srngararasaprabandhadipika*)

Bhugnaka Group – Kama Sutra
Suvarnanabha has a posture-sequence
derived from *Bhugnaka* (Rising),
in which pose the lady, lying on her back,
lifts both thighs high
and keeps them pressed tightly together.

If she crosses her raised thighs,
the posture changes to *Piditaka* (the Squeeze).
If, alternatively, she puts her feet
on your shoulders,
it becomes *Jrimbhitaka* (the Yawning).

If both her feet are at your chest
and you press her knees down on her breasts,
it is *Utpiditaka* (the High Squeeze).
And if now she stretches one leg at a time,
it is *Ardhapiditaka* (the Half Squeeze).

If, in *Jrimbhitaka*, she releases a foot
and slowly stretches her leg to its full length,
pulls it back and stretches
her other leg along the bed as far as it can go,
it is *Venudaritaka* (Splitting Bamboo).

If she places one heel on your head,
keeping her other leg stretched out straight
and alternates as above,
it is called *Shulachita* (the Spit-roast):
she is the spit and you are the roast.

Lataveshta, the Clinging Creeper, mentioned in two medieval texts, is the natural line arising from the *Pidita-Veshtita* sequence given in *Kama Sutra*. Although the painting has some Kashmiri features, it is probably a product of the Delhi *bazaars*. It is interesting to think that paintings such as this were still being made when Burton and Arbuthnot sat down with their pandits to make their translation of Vatsyayana's text. *Delhi, Bazaar style, nineteenth century*

Bhugnaka Group – Medieval Texts
When, lifting her feet high,
you kneel between her parted thighs
and make love, vigorously
caressing and kneading her two breasts,
it is *Ardhasamputa* (Half Jewel-case).
(Ratimanjari)

When your skilful lady lifts crossed thighs
and places both her heels
on one of your shoulders, her buttocks
being passionately struck by your penis driving
rapidly, it is *Nagara* (the Town Way).
(Panchasayaka)

When, lying on her back,
the lovely woman lifts her feet to your shoulders
and keeps them criss-crossing
in rhythm with your swift thrusting,
it is *Vanshadaraka* (the Bamboo Poles).
(Smaradipika)

If she lies on her back,
her thighs clamped about your waist,
and you sit close to enter her,
it is *Nagara* (the Town Way),
an especial favourite with the *chitrini*[2].
(Ananga Ranga)

If you place the two feet
of the lotus-eyed one in your lap
and make love while
embracing her around the neck,
it is *Ratilila* (Aphrodite's Game).
(Ratikallolini)

Clasp her feet together
and hold them pressed tight to your heart,
let your other hand wander
the valleys and peaks of her breast-country:
this is *Priyatoshana* (Lovers' Delight)
(Smaradipika)

If now she rocks back and forth,
pushing with her feet against your chest,
clasping your hands in hers
as you beat wholeheartedly upon her *yoni*,
it is *Prenkha* (the Swing).
(Ratirahasya/Ratimanjari)

When, lying back, she lifts
one foot to your shoulder
and you cradle her other foot in one palm,
your free hand stroking her breasts,
it is *Ekapada* (One Foot).
(Smaradipika)

Her left leg stretched straight,
she lifts her right leg and pulls it back
until her toes touch the mattress behind her head.
Make love, keeping your weight
off her body: this is *Traivikrama* (the Stride).
(Ananga Ranga)

Lying side by side in bed,
raise one of her feet to your heart,
leaving her other leg stretched out straight:
this is *Vinasana* (the Lute),
a posture adored by experienced women.
(Ananga Ranga)

Lying on your sides,
your bodies caressing from lips to toes,
lift one foot to the heart
of the lovely-eyed woman and pierce her *yoni*:
this is *Ratibana* (Love's Arrow).
(Ratikallolini)

Karkata-Yoga Group – Kama Sutra
If, like a crab folding its legs
across its belly,
your lover brings her feet to your navel,
soles pressed flat together,
the posture is called *Karkata* (the Crab).

Karkata-Yoga Group – Medieval Texts
When she lies on her back
with limbs outflung like a crab's
and curls her arms and legs to draw you to her,
squeezing you tightly,
it is known as *Karkata* (the Crab).

Now seize her wrists and uncurl her limbs,
your tongue caressing
her nipples and the place between her thighs;
embrace her, squashing her breasts
against your chest: this is *Ghattita* (Caressing).
(Srngararasaprabandhadipika)

If she lies on her back
and you embrace her,
passing your arms beneath your knees
to ply her fearlessly,
it is *Nagapasha* (the Cobra Knot).
(Smaradipika)

When your lover passes her arms
under her raised thighs
and twines her fingers together behind your neck,
pulling your face down to be kissed,
it is *Phanabhritpasha* (the Knot of the Hooded One).
(Ratiratnapradipika)

---

2. See p. 36

The inscription to this lavishly ornamented miniature describes
the lovers as being in the *Mudita* (Gladdening) posture, which
results in great pleasure. The posture can develop into
Shulachita, or *Jrimbhitaka*. Or, if the lady draws up and extends
her legs alternately, it would become the most celebrated of
Kama Sutra's postures, the *Venudaritaka*, or Splitting Bamboo.
Jaipur, mid nineteenth century

Your lips upon her lips,
your arms to her arms,
your thighs laid along her thighs,
your chest crushing her breasts:
this is *Kanakakshaya* (Wealth Destroyer).
(*Smaradipika*)

Each of you with arms and legs extended
in the full *kaurmasana*[3],
she below, you above,
lips, arms and thighs meeting, hands joined:
this is *Kaurma* (the Tortoise).
(*Ratiratnapradipika*)

She lies back with her feet placed
high on the opposing thighs;
run your hands over her body, enter her suddenly
and pleasure her with hard strokes:
this is *Padmasana* (the Lotus Position).
(*Ratimanjari*)

When lovers lie on their backs,
their lovely limbs
flower-yoked (each with feet folded in the lotus)
in the middle of the bed,
it is known as *Vriksha* (the Tree).
(*Srngararasaprabandhadipika*)

Lying back, she lifts her legs
and catches hold of her two big toes,
gripping them tightly,
while you sit between her raised, parted thighs
to embrace her neck and make love.

This is the famous *Sanyama*
(the Controlled),
highly recommended in the *Kama Sutra*
of Mallanaga Vatsyayana
and by others who were expert in the art of love.
(*Ratiratnapradipika*)

Lying on her back, your lover
lays her knees to either side of her brow,
heels well apart on the bed,
spreading wide the proud triple crest of her *yoni*:
this is *Shulanka* (Shiva's Trident).
(*Ratiratnapradipika*)

Sitting Positions

Padmasana Group – Kama Sutra
When the left foot is placed high
upon the right thigh
and the right foot high on the left thigh,
this love posture
is *Padmasana* (the Lotus Position)[4].

Padmasana Group – Medieval Texts
If your wife, placing her left foot
upon her right thigh
and vice versa, raises her crossed legs
up towards her stomach,
it is *Padmasana* (the Lotus Position).

But if only one of her feet
is folded in this way
and tucked high on the opposing thigh
while her other leg is stretched out straight,
it is *Ardhapadmasana* (the Half Lotus).
(*Ananga Ranga*)

When you sit erect in the lotus pose,
hands clasping your feet,
and your lover places her feet on your thighs,
her breasts piercing your chest,
and makes love, it is *Matsya* (the Fish).

If, clasping you tightly in this embrace,
she places her feet on the bed
and slowly twists her spine to face away from you
without breaking your union,
it is *Jvalamukhi* (the Flame Faced).
(*Srngararasaprabandhadipika*)

If, seated erect on the bed,
she folds her feet in prayer at her navel
and makes love, supported
by your strong thighs gripping her waist,
it is *Kauliraka* (Kauli *tantra-yoga*)[5] .

And if, during *Kauliraka*,
you push with your feet against the bed,
swaying your young bride gently back and forth,
it is *Prenkhi* (the Swing) –
a way through lovemaking to perfect peace.
(*Ratiratnapradipika*)

---

3. A *yoga* posture named for its resemblance to a tortoise with tucked-in head and limbs. It is Plate 363 in Iyengar's *Light on Yoga* (pp. 288–291). *Tantrics* may have used it to obtain the effect described in *Bhagavad Gita*: 'When, again, as a tortoise draws its limbs in on all sides, he withdraws his senses from the objects of sense, and then his understanding is well-poised' (II:58). According to Iyengar it also tones the spine and the abdominal organs.

4. The most famous of all *yoga* postures, the best one for meditation. *Hatha Yoga Pradipika* says: 'Assuming *padmasana*, and having placed the palms one upon the other, fix the chin firmly upon the breast and, contemplating upon *Brahman*, frequently contract the anus and raise the *apana* up; by similar

contraction of the throat force the *prana* down. By this the *yogi* obtains unequalled knowledge through the favour of *Kundalini*, which is roused by this process.'

5. The Kaulis or Kaulas (see Glossary) were a *tantric* sect which practised the left-hand *shakta* ritual, or ritual sexual intercourse. Cannabis-laced drinks were served with fish, pork, wine and cereals. The *Kaulavalinimaya* explains that: 'All the men become Shiva and all the women the Goddess. The pork becomes Shiva and the wine Shakti. They take the five foods, consecrating the twelve cups of wine with evocations, and unite in sexual intercourse.' The ritual was meant to unite the blissful *tantric* with the universal Shakti, or life-force.

This rather difficult looking posture must owe something of its strangeness to the painter's use of perspective. It appears to be a variant of what *Ratiratnapradipika* describes as *Shulanka*, which gets its name because, when seen from above, the man's stiff body and the woman's raised legs resemble the three prongs of a trident.
Mewar, c.1760

Kaurma Group – Kama Sutra

If you're seated in a tight embrace
and she wheels around,
without breaking the rhythm of your lovemaking,
to embrace you from behind,
it is the virtuoso *Paravrittaka* (the Turnaround).

Paravrittaka is also possible
in certain of the rear-entry positions,
but it is just as difficult
to master, and requires as much
hard practice as the seated version.

Kaurma Group – Medieval Texts

Seated, mouth to mouth,
arms against arms, thighs pressed to thighs:
this is *Kaurma* (the Tortoise).
If the lovers' thighs, still joined, are raised,
it is *Paravartita* (Turning).

(Ananga Ranga)

If within the cave of her thighs
you sit rotating your hips like a black bee[6],
it is *Markata* (the Monkey).
And if, in this pose, you turn away from her,
it is *Marditaka* (Crushing Spices).

(Ratiratnapradipika)

She sits with raised thighs,
her feet placed either side of your waist;
linga enters *yoni*;
you rain hard blows upon her body:
this is *Kshudgara* (Striking).

(Ratimanjari)

When your wife sits
with both knees drawn tight to her body
and you mirror this posture,
it is known to experts in the art of love
as *Yugmapada* (the Foot Yoke).

(Ananga Ranga)

Seated erect, the lovely girl
folds one leg to her body
and stretches the other along the bed,
while you mirror her actions:
this is *Yugmapada* (the Foot Yoke).

(Ratirahasya)

If, with left leg extended,
she encircles your waist with her right leg,
laying its ankle across her left thigh,
and you do the same,
it is *Svastika* (the Swastika)[7].

(Srngararasaprabandhadipika)

Sitting face to face in bed,
her breasts pressed tight against your chest,
let each of you lock heels
behind the other's waist,
and lean back clasping one another's wrists.

Now, set the swing gently in motion,
your beloved, in pretended fear,
clinging to your body with her flawless limbs,
cooing and moaning with pleasure:
this is *Dolita* (the Swing).

(Srngararasaprabandhadipika)

If, seated face to face,
your toes caress the lovely woman's nipples,
her feet press your chest
and you make love holding each other's hands
it is *Kaurma* (the Tortoise).

(Srngararasaprabandhadipika)

If, sitting facing her,
you grasp her ankles and fasten them like a chain
behind your neck, and she
grips her toes as you make love,
it is the delightful *Padma* (the Lotus).

(Srngararasaprabandhadipika)

Seated, the lady raises
one foot to point vertically over her head
and steadies it with her hands,
offering up her *yoni* for lovemaking:
this is *Mayura* (the Peacock).

(Srngararasaprabandhadipika)

Sitting erect, grip your lover's waist
and pull her on to you,
your loins continuously leaping together
with a sound like the flapping of elephants' ears:
this is *Kirtibandha* (the Knot of Fame).

(Panchasayaka)

---

6. The bee (*bhramara*) was observed to rotate its abdomen as it dived headfirst into a flower to gather pollen, hence the simile. The word for 'wheel' derives from the same root (*bhram*, to revolve) and the posture known as the Bee (see p.76) is often translated as the Wheel.

7. An ancient good-luck talisman based on the symbolism of a cross whirling sun-wise. The Nazis used it the wrong way round, whirling widdershins, and the Indian pandits always said that this sacrilege would doom them.

A prince of Jodhpur and his wife in a difficult variant of *Bandhura*, the Curved Knot.
Did the lady ever amuse herself with some of the priceless absurdities of the
Jodhpur treasury, like the pair of diamond eyebrows that hook, like spectacles, over
the ears? And was she one of those who left her handprints on the wall of the Loha
Gate of Jodhpur Fort as she went out to immolate herself on the funeral pyre of her
husband, the Maharaja? *Jodhpur, early eighteenth century.*

Kneeling between her thighs,
tickle her breasts and under her arms,
call her 'my lovely darling'
and print deep nailmarks around her nipples:
thus *Jaya* (Victory) is expounded.

(Srngararasaprabandhadipika)

Bandha Group – Medieval Texts

When you sit with your arms
flung around the neck of the lovely girl,
and she presses both palms
flat against your thudding heart,
it is *Nagara* (the Town Way).

(Smaradipika)

Clinging to one another's necks,
drinking sweet kisses
from each other's bud-like lower lips,
thighs tightly meshed,
making love: this is *Pallava* (the New Leaf).

(Srngararasaprabandhadipika)

When, seated, you pass your arms
under her lifted thighs,
clasping your fingers tightly behind her neck,
and make love to her,
it is *Sanyama* (the Controlled).

(Ananga Ranga)

If, threading their hands
under their own knees
and each firmly grasping the other's shoulders,
the couple couple,
it is known as *Bandhura* (the Curved Knot).

(Ratikallolini)

If, seated facing you,
your lover works her arms under her thighs
to lace her fingers behind your neck,
and you do exactly the same,
it is *Bandhurita* (the Curved Knot).

(Ananga Ranga)

If, with her arms round your neck
and your arms between hers clasping her neck,
you make love clinging together,
it is, says Kalyana Malla, Prince of Poets[8],
Phanipasha (the Cobra Knot).

(Ananga Ranga)

Standing Positions

From Kama Sutra

And now for the love postures
with which sculptors adorn our temple walls[9].
When a couple make love standing,
or leaning against a wall or a pillar,
it is called *Sthita* (Steadied).

When the woman sits in her lover's
cradled hands, her arms around his neck,
thighs gripping his waist,
her feet pushing back and forth against a wall,
it is *Avalambitaka* (Suspended).

From the Medieval Texts

When, catching and crushing your lover
in the cage of your arms,
you force her knees apart with yours
and sink slowly into her,
it is *Dadhyayataka* (Churning Curds).

(Panchasayaka)

When she leans against a wall,
planting her feet as widely apart as possible,
and you enter the cave
between her thighs, eager for lovemaking,
it is *Sammukha* (Face-to-face).

(Ratiratnapradipika)

If, as you lean against a wall,
your lady twines her thighs around yours,
locks her feet to your knees,
and clasps your neck, making love
very passionately, it is *Dola* (the Swing).

(Smaradipika)

When your lover draws up one leg,
allowing the heel
to nestle just behind your knee,
and you make love, embracing her forcefully,
it is *Traivikrama* (the Stride)[10].

(Ratiratnapradipika)

If you catch one of her knees
firmly in your hand
and stand making love with her
while her hands explore and caress your body,
it is *Tripadam* (the Tripod).

(Panchasayaka)

---

8. See Glossary

9. See p. 46, note 2

---

10. The name refers to the three strides with which Vishnu crossed the world (see Glossary under Bali). The posture is often called *Harivikrama* (Vishnu's Stride). In paintings the striding Vishnu is shown with one leg raised vertically above his head, which gives an indication of what the related *Traivikrama* posture (see *Bhugnaka* group) involved.

Nepalese *tantrics* in a simple standing posture. They wear
consecrated amulets and the man has a Gurkha hat. Nepal was
one of the strongholds of the *tantric* tradition and many
Nepalese temples – like rustic Khajurahos – are embellished
with gaudily painted woodcarvings of amorous couples. The
couple in this old painting regard each other not as man and
woman, but as embodiments of Parvati and Shiva. Their
favoured sexual postures are usually *yoga*-derived (see
Kauliraka, p. 64) and they will use *mantras* and breathing
techniques to prevent themselves coming to orgasm and so
dissipating the *kundalini* energy with which their bodies are
charged. *Nepal, c.1700*

If she raises one leg
and you catch hold of her little foot,
caressing her breasts
and telling her how much you love her,
it is *Ekapada* (One Foot).
(*Srngararasaprabandhadipika*)

Her foot pressed to your heart,
your arms encircling and supporting her,
lean back against the wall
and enjoy the lovely girl:
this is *Veshta* (the Encircling).
(*Smaradipika*)

She stands against the wall,
lotus-hands on hips,
long, lovely fingers reaching to her navel.
Cup her foot in your palm
and let your free hand caress her angel's limbs.

Put your arm round her neck
and enjoy her as she leans there at her ease.
Vatsyayana and others
who knew the art of love in its great days
called this posture *Tala* (the Palm).
(*Ratiratnapradipika*)

If you lean back to a wall
and your lover, clinging to your neck,
places both her feet
in your palms and thus makes love,
this is *Dvitala* (Two Palms).
(*Ratirahasya*)

If you lift your lover
by passing your elbows under her knees
and gripping her buttocks
while she hangs fearfully from your neck,
it is *Janukurpara* (the Knee Elbow).
(*Ratiratnapradipika*)

Your wife grips your neck
and locks her legs around your waist:
this is *Kirti* (Fame) – a posture
not described in *Kama Sutra* or *Ratirahasya*.
Never try it with heavy girls.
(*Ananga Ranga*)

Rear-entry Positions

From Kama Sutra
If she stands four-footed
with both palms laid flat on the carpet
and you mount her like a bull,
caressing her back instead of her breasts,
it is *Dhenuka* (the Milch Cow).

It's also fun to mimic animals
like dogs, deer and goats,
copying their movements and their cries:
to attack abruptly, like the ass;
or arch your backs like two voluptuous cats.

Pounce like a tiger; haul yourself
slowly along her back like a great solemn tusker;
grind like a wild-boar;
mount her proudly, like a stallion:
these games teach new tricks, even to experts.

From the Medieval Texts
She bends well forward and grips
the bedstead, her buttocks raised high;
cup your hands to serpents' hoods
and squeeze her jar-shaped breasts together:
this is *Dhenuka* (the Milch Cow).
(*Srngararasaprabandhadipika*)

If you mount her like a dog,
gripping her waist,
and she twists round to gaze into your face,
experts in the art of love say
it is *Svanaka* (the Dog).
(*Srngararasaprabandhadipika*)

If the lady, eager for love,
goes on all fours, humping her back like a doe,
and you enjoy her from behind,
rutting as though you'd lost all human nature,
it is *Harina* (the Deer).
(*Panchasayaka*)

When, with lotus-feet
set well-apart on the ground, she bends,
placing a hand upon each thigh,
and you take her from the rear,
it is *Gardabha* (the Ass).
(*Srngararasaprabandhadipika*)

A demanding variation of *Janukurpara*, the Knee Elbow position. The girl's arms, in this painting, instead of being round her lover's neck, are clasped about his waist. The Kotah love of vegetation is expressed by the banana leaves over the garden wall. Notice the blue and white Chinese vases standing in the niches that all old Indian houses have in their walls. *Kotah, late eighteenth century*

If she lies on her stomach
and you seize her ankles in one hand,
lift them high and make love,
tilting her chin back with your other hand,
it is *Marjara* (the Cat).
(Srngararasaprabandhadipika)

She lies on her front,
grasping her ankles in her own hands
and pulling them up behind her:
this difficult posture is known to experts
as *Mallaka* (the Wrestler).
(Panchasayaka)

When your mistress lays
breasts, arms and forehead to the carpet,
raising her buttocks high,
and you guide your penis into her *yoni*,
it is *Aibha* (the Elephant).
(Ratirahasya)

You lift her ankles high;
she draws up
and extends her legs as though she were
crawling through the air:
this is *Hastika* (the Elephant).
(Srngararasaprabandhadipika)

She stands on palms and feet;
you stand behind her
and lift one of her feet to your shoulder,
enjoying the lovely girl:
this is *Traivikrama* (the Stride).
(Panchasayaka)

Seize her feet and lift them high
(like a wheelbarrow),
drive your penis into her *yoni*
and pleasure her with vigorous strokes:
this is *Kulisha* (the Thunderbolt).
(Smaradipika)

You kneel, as in archery,
take her on your lap
and bend her forward till her breasts
are pressed to her thighs:
this is *Ekabandha* (One Knot).
(Smaradipika)

Lying on her side, facing away,
the fawn-eyed girl
offers you her buttocks
and your penis penetrates the house of love:
this is *Nagabandha* (the Elephant).
(Panchasayaka)

---

11. Sacred texts

12. See Glossary under Ahalya

13. See Glossary

Exotic Lovemaking – Kama Sutra

Suvarnanabha says it's delightful
to make love in deep water;
the most complex knots, twists and bends,
yoga and temple postures
are easily and pleasurably mastered.

But the advice is worthless,
says Vatsyayana: it contradicts the teachings
of holy sages and the *smritis*[11]
and is forbidden by Gotama, who says: 'the couple
who copulate in water will be damned.'[12]

When you make a threesome in bed
with two wives who are fond of one another,
it is *Sanghataka* (the Pair).
If you pleasure many of your ladies at once,
it is *Goyuthika* (the Herd).

When, like a herd of wild elephants
escaping the summer's heat,
you dally with several of your wives
in some shaded river pool,
it is known as *Varikriditaka* (the Water Game).

Similarly, you may play the part
of a ram or a stag,
strutting among his herd of concubines.
Women who like to enjoy
two or more lovers can also play these games.

In the mountain country of the Nagas
and in Balkh and Strirajya[13],
the frustrated ladies of the royal households
often smuggle young men
into their harems and keep them hidden there.

A queen will sit on one man's lap
while another enters her
and still others cover her body with kisses,
nailmarks and lovebites,
taking turns with her until she's satisfied.

But in most civilized countries
these orgiastic sessions are the prerogative
of courtesans and prostitutes.
Only very rarely does one hear
of royal princesses servicing the court's *sirdars*[14].

The peoples of the southern countries
have a fondness for buggery
and practise it freely with both men and women.
Oral sex and role reversal
will be discussed in later chapters.

---

14. The senior courtiers. Diwan Jarmani Das, former prime minister of Kapurthala state, has written two books which deal with the orgiastic goings-on at various pre-Independence Indian courts.

To judge from the tales told by ex-ministers of various pre-independence Indian courts, it has been common ever since Vatsyayana's day for princes to be entertained by several of their ladies at once. The king in this painting is Maharaja Ram Singh of Kotah (1827–65), but the picture was probably intended as a piece of discreet flattery. Vatsyayana calls this situation *Goyuthika*, the Herd. *Kotah, c.1840–50*

ROLE REVERSAL

First, the ways to arouse and satisfy
a difficult lover.
Start by inveigling her into lying on your bed,
and distract her with sweet words
before slyly loosening the knot of her skirt.

If she tries to stop you, kiss her
pleadingly, until she's troubled by desire.
When your penis stiffens and rises
make sure she can feel it
gently nudging and caressing her limbs.

If it's your first time together,
she's bound to object
when you try to touch her between her thighs
and will squeeze them together:
you must caress them until they ease apart again.

Now lull her suspicions by letting
your hands seem more interested in her breasts,
throat, arms, waist and hips.
This is especially important with virgins,
who take a great deal of caressing.

If she's an experienced woman
she'll have seen straight through this subterfuge,
but you should seize her hair and turn
her mouth to you for kisses
and leave fresh lovebites on her cheeks.

If your sweetheart is a virgin
she will by now have shyly closed her eyes,
which means you must work blind;
for written in the beautiful eyes of women,
if you can read it, is one of love's great secrets.

When a caress is especially thrilling
her eyes will roll upwards
in ecstasy, or so runs Suvarnanabha's theory.
Let her eyes choose the caress,
and your lady very quickly becomes passionate.

When she is ready for lovemaking
her limbs will seem heavy
and her movements slow, languorous;
her eyes close and she presses
her mound of Venus shamelessly to your groin.

You can tell her orgasm is near
when her arms begin to shake,
her body grows slippery with sweat,
she bites and scratches
and her legs jerk and kick out uncontrollably.

If you reach your climax while she's
still hovering on the brink,
she clings to you, will not let you pull away
and in her desperate passion
continues to thrust violently after you're still.

To make sure this doesn't happen
you should prepare her,
before lovemaking, by shaping your fingers
to an elephant's trunk and playing
in her *yoni* until she is thoroughly wet.

During lovemaking, ten types of blow
may be struck with the penis,
but of these only *Upasripta* (Natural),
which is instinctive even to untutored cowherds,
results in full clitoral stimulation.

It is a gentle forward stroke
which may be varied for depth and speed,
allowing a subtlety, rhythm
and spontaneity which
the other nine each lack to some degree.

If you grasp your penis and move it
in circles inside her *yoni,*
it is *Manthana* (Churning).
When you strike sharply down into the *yoni,*
it is *Hula* (the Double-bladed Knife).

If, when her hips are raised by a pillow,
you strike a rising blow,
it is *Avamardana* (Rubbing).
If you hold your penis pressed breathlessly
to her womb it is *Piditaka* (Pressing).

If you withdraw completely
and then strike her violently to the womb,
it is *Nirghata* (the Buffet).
Continuous pressure on one side of her *yoni*
is *Varahaghata* (the Boar's Blow).

If you thrust wildly in every direction,
like a bull tossing its horns,
it is *Vrishaghata* (the Bull's Blow).
Quivering in her *yoni* is *Chatakavilasa*
(Sparrow Sport), which usually heralds orgasm.

The involuntary shuddering of orgasm
is called *Samputa* (the Jewel Case).
But no two women make love quite the same way,
so orchestrate your rhythms
to the moods and colours of each lover's *raga*[1].

---

1. Emotions. The various scales of Indian music are also called
ragas. The musical metaphor suggests the flowing,
improvisational nature of lovemaking as taught in the love
texts.

This painting, of the Jodhpur maharaja enjoying two of his ladies at the same time, clearly illustrates the Indian preference for round-limbed, slightly plump girls. The *trivalli*, three faint creases about the waist, was the supreme sign of beauty. The king and the lady who now claims his attention are in the *Kshudgara* posture (see p. 66) which calls for vigorous action, hence his use of the *Hula* stroke described opposite. *Jodhpur, early nineteenth century*

Role Reversal

If long lovemaking exhausts you
before your lover has reached her orgasm,
you should allow her
to roll you over on your back
and sit astride you, taking the initiative.

If the posture gives her deep pleasure,
or you enjoy its novelty,
she may transpose into it as a matter of course,
taking great care, however,
not to expel the *linga* from the temple of love.

A skilled lover will reverse roles
without breaking the rolling rhythms of love.
If you've already made love once,
she can easily arouse you to a second bout
by taking the man's role from the start.

Consider: she climbs upon you,
the flowers dropping from her tousled hair,
her giggles turning to gasps;
every time she bends to kiss your lips
her nipples pierce your chest.

As her hips begin to churn,
her head, flung back, bobs ever faster;
she scratches, pummels you with small fists,
fastens her teeth in your neck,
doing unto you what you've so often done to her.

She cries, drunk as a conqueror,
'You ground me down, now you're humiliated!',
but orgasm takes her abruptly,
closing her beautiful eyes;
she nuzzles shyly to you, once more a woman

When she takes the man's role,
your lady has the choice
of three famous lovemaking techniques:
Samdamsha (the Tongs),
Bhramara (the Bee) and *Prenkholita* (the Swing).

If she uses the Mare's Trick[2],
gripping your penis with her *yoni's* vice,
squeezing and stroking it,
holding it inside her for a hundred heart-beats,
it is known as *Samdamsha* (the Tongs).

If, drawing up her feet,
she revolves her hips so that your penis
circles deep within her *yoni,*
you arching your body to help her,
it is *Bhramara* (the Bee), which needs practice.

If she now swings her hips
in wide circles and makes figures-of-eight,
swaying upon your body
as though she were riding on a seesaw,
it is *Prenkholita* (the Swing).

When her passion has ebbed,
she should rest, bending forward to lay
her forehead upon yours
without disturbing your yoked bodies:
it won't be very long before desire stirs again.

From the Medieval Texts
Catching your penis, the lady
with dark eyes like upturned lotus petals
guides it into her *yoni,*
clings to you and shakes her buttocks:
this is *Charunarikshita* (Lovely Lady in Control).
                                        (*Ratikallolini*)

Enthroned on your penis,
she places both hands on the bed
and makes love, while you
press your two hands to her thudding heart:
this is *Lilasana* (Seat of Sport).
                                        (*Smaradipika*)

She sits upright upon you,
her head thrown back like a rearing mare,
bringing her feet together
on the bed to one side of your body:
this is *Hansabandha* (the Swan).
                                (*Srngararasaprabandhadipika*)

---

2. See p. 60

The couple in this very striking miniature are in the posture described as
Charunarikshita by the love text *Ratikallolini*. The contrast between the lady's pale
body and the rich red of the carpet is both unusual and effective. Here again, the
treatment of the face echoes certain characteristics of the earlier Guler style. *Pahari,
Sikh School, mid nineteenth century*

The young woman has one foot
on your heart and the other on the bed.
Bold, saucy women adore this posture,
which is known to the world
as *Upavitika* (the Sacred Thread)[3].

(*Panchasayaka*)

If, with one of her feet
clasped in your hand
and the second placed upon your shoulder,
your young lady enjoys you,
it is *Viparitaka* (Reversed).

(*Smaradipika*)

If your lover, seated above you
with feet lotus-crossed
and her body held erect and still,
makes love to you,
it is known as *Yugmapada* (the Foot Yoke).

(*Ratiratnapradipika*)

Seated above you with her feet
folded in the lotus-pose,
she threads her arms through the foot-lock
and lays her palms flat on the ground:
this is *Kukkuta* (the Cockerel).

(*Srngararasaprabandhadipika*)

If, sitting astride you,
she twists to bring one foot to your thigh,
and draws up the other foot
to place it on your chest,
this is called *Viparitaka* (Reversed).

(*Ratimanjari*)

If she sits astride you,
facing your feet,
brings both her feet up to your thighs,
and works her hips frantically,
it is known as *Hansa-lila* (Swan Sport).

(*Smaradipika*)

Your lover places one foot
on your ankle, lodges
her other foot just above your knee,
and rides you, swinging and rotating her hips:
this is *Garuda* (Garuda)[4].

(*Srngararasaprabandhadipika*)

If you lie flat on your back
with legs stretched out
and your lover sits astride you, facing away
and grasping your feet,
it is called *Vrisha* (the Bull).

(*Srngararasaprabandhadipika*)

With her limbs entwined in yours,
kissing and playing
a hundred delightful lovegames,
the darling girl usurps your rightful role:
this is *Valli* (the Creeper).

(*Srngararasaprabandhadipika*)

Clasping each other's hands,
you lie sprawled like two starfish making love,
her breasts stabbing your chest,
her thighs stretched out along yours:
this is *Devabandha* (the Coitus of the Gods).

(*Srngararasaprabandhadipika*)

Lying upon you, your beloved
moves round like a wheel,
pressing hands one after the other on the bed,
kissing your body as she circles:
experts call this *Chakrabandha* (the Wheel).

(*Srngararasaprabandhadipika*)

If, by means of some contraption,
your lover suspends herself above you,
places your *linga* in her *yoni*
and pulleys herself up and down upon it,
it is *Utkalita* (the Orissan)[5].

(*Ananga Ranga*)

Concluding Remarks – Kama Sutra
Even the shyest, most reserved woman,
adept at hiding her feelings
and pretending she's untroubled by desire,
can't help showing her passion
when she's seated making love astride a man.

But never play these games
with a woman who is menstruating,
or who has just given birth,
nor with a deer woman,
nor a pregnant or excessively heavy girl.

---

3. The cotton thread of nine strands with which *brahmin* boys
are invested during their initiation as priests.

4. The mythological bird which was the god Vishnu's mount.

5. *Utkalita*. Burton's *Ananga Ranga* has *utthita* (standing), which
makes no sense. See Glossary for Orissa.

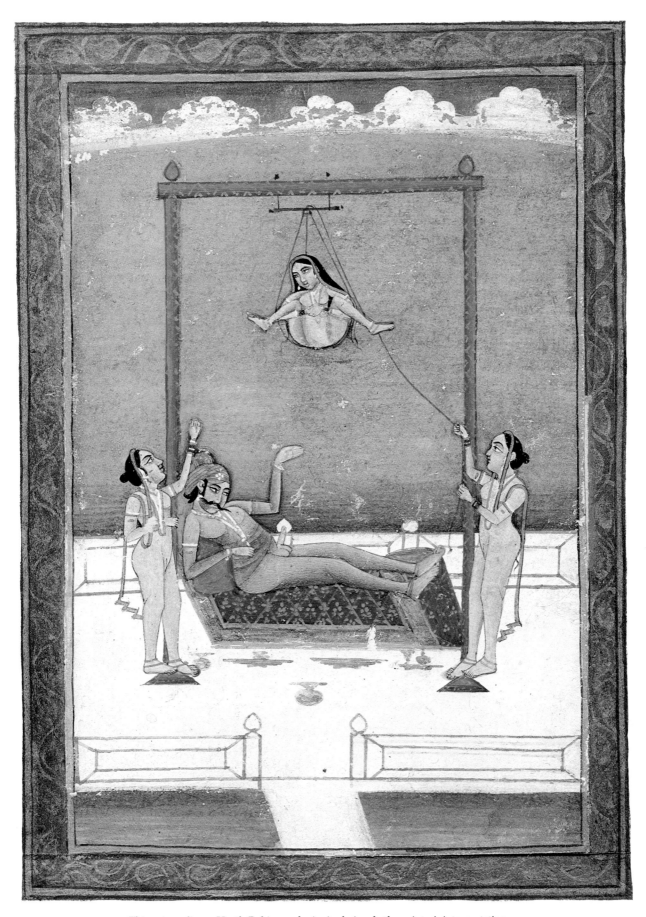

This extraordinary Heath-Robinson device is obviously the painter's interpretation of the posture called *Utkalita* in *Ananga Ranga*. The fact that Kalyana Malla derived his information from an Orissan source is interesting because the favourite task of Orissan painters and engravers was to illustrate the *Kama Sutra* and it is possible that Vatsyayana's *Prenkholita* was the original of this posture. *Jaipur, nineteenth century*

LOVEBLOWS AND LOVECRIES

Since lovemaking, by its nature,
is something of a battle between the sexes,
the various loveblows,
which can greatly enhance pleasure,
are considered worth discussing in the love texts.

Four blows – *Apahasta* (the Backhand),
Prasritaka (the Hood), *Mushti* (the Fist)
and *Samatala* (the Palm) –
may be used on her head, shoulders, back, sides
and in the space between her breasts.

Your lover, naturally, will feel pain
when you strike her,
but the cries that come bubbling from her throat,
if you can recognize each type,
will quickly tell you how far she is aroused.

Hinkara is a sharply indrawn breath,
like a sudden start.
Stanita is a deeper, more resonant sound,
beaten on the kettledrums of her lungs.
Kujita is a gentle cooing, like that of doves.

Rudita is the throaty sobbing of a woman
coming to her orgasm.
Sutkrita is her harsh panting.
Dutkrita is a choked rattle, like bamboo splitting.
Phutkrita is like a berry falling in water.

Sitkrita are the words and sounds
your blows force from her,
exclamations of pain fighting with pleasure.
The sequence, which should be learned,
shades from pleasure to pain to deeper pleasure.

At first she'll sob things like 'mother!'
'stop!' 'let go!' 'enough!'
'let me alone!' 'oh, I'm dying!',
but the breaths now fluttering in her throat
soon turn to wordless cries.

Her first shy cries may sound to you
like sobbing doves,
the cuckoo's call climbing in the leaves,
woodpigeons' drowsy sighing,
the shrill shriek of her parrot in its cage.

But soon your lady, moaning like a black bee,
piping like a startled moorhen,
uttering low harsh cries that sound
like wild geese and wild ducks calling on the wing,
ends yammering shameless as a quail[1].

When she is lying below you on the bed
you should slap back-handed between her breasts.
At first, strike her gently,
but as your passion mounts let your blows
fall faster and harder: this is *Apahasta*.

Expertly struck, this blow
will draw from her a *raga* composed of drumming,
cooing and sobbing cries.
If you hurt her she should abuse you angrily,
returning blow for blow.

The lovecries need not be made
in a particular order:
her performance should be entirely improvised.
But each blow you strike
should not fail to elicit a cry of pleasure.

When, because she gets no satisfaction
from the Backhand and asks you
to try another kind of blow, you strike her head
with your fingers curled to a snake-hood,
it is *Prasritaka* (the Hood).

Your aim is to arouse her
to such passion that her cries of '*Hare Rama*'[2]
catch in her throat, turning
to a roulade of closed and open vowels
and ending in strangulated sobs.

You should tease her
by mimicking her more extraordinary cries,
making her laugh and then
spurring her with your nails and teeth
to even more extravagant effects.

When you feel your climax approaching,
strike her thighs and sides
with the flat, even palmstrokes of *Samatala*.
Time this accurately and you'll hear
the wild goose and quail calling her to orgasm.

---

1. The Sanskrit of this bird sequence displays great mastery of rhythm and assonance, which are used to suggest the woman's mounting excitement:
ambārthāha-shabdāha-vāranārthā-mōkshanārthāschalamārtha-stē-tē-chārtha-yōgāt-pārāvat-parabhrit-hārīt-shuk-madhukara-dātyūha-hansa-kārandava-lāvaka-virutāni-sītkrita-bhūyishtāni-vikalpashaha-

prayunjīt – the consonants topple into one another like a row of dominoes.

2. A common expletive. Its nearest English equivalent would be 'Jesus Christ!'

The couple are making love in what Vatsyayana describes as the *Sthita* position (see
p. 68), and the man's left hand is poised to deliver a blow in the *Apahasta* (Backhand)
manner. Other paintings in this series show a man having his turban tied by an
attendant while he is making love to a lady and a pair of lovers in the countryside
disturbed by an archer shooting at wild ducks. *Mewar, late eighteenth century*

Men, by nature, are tougher,
fiercer and more violent than women,
who are delicate and shy,
hence it is usually the man who strikes
and the woman who cries out.

But if passion overwhelms her
or she is excited by an unusual love posture
or it is her country's custom,
the woman may rain blows upon her lover.
However this rarely happens.

Four other blows are sometimes used:
Kila (Wedge) on the bosom,
Kartari (Scissors) on the head,
Vidvam (Skewer) on the cheeks
and *Samdanshikam* (Pincers) on the breasts[3].

These dangerous blows are especially
popular in southern countries.
Often one will see, on the breasts of southerners
and their wives, marks
left by hard blows made in the *Kila* style.

But the customs of the south
are not to be aped by curious northerners.
Vatsyayana says these blows
are un-Aryan and not fit for gentlefolk,
who ought to regard such violence with contempt.

Indeed, there is no doubt
that practices which can lead to broken limbs,
disfigurement and death,
should scarcely be condoned, even in places
which refuse to regard them as utterly barbaric.

It's no secret that the Chola king
recently killed a courtesan called Chitrasena
by striking her *Kila* fashion .
King Shatkarni of the Kuntalas killed Malyavati,
his great queen, with the Scissors .

Naradeva, Commander-in-Chief
of the Pandya armies,
whose left hand was deformed,
once struck in the *Vidvam* way at a dancing girl
and, missing his aim, put out her eye .

But when men are inflamed by passion
they give little thought
either to the *shastras* or to the consequences
of their mad violence:
passion itself causes these calamities.

Nothing addles wits faster than sex:
the cravings and fantasies
that float unbidden into a man's imagination
when he's making love are weirder,
by far, even than the grotesqueries of his dreams.

Just as a horse at full gallop
doesn't notice the ditches, pits and walls
which line his route,
the fury of passion blinds lovers
to the harm that nails, teeth and fists can do.

Try always to remember, therefore,
that your lover is much weaker than you are
and passion is much stronger.
Furthermore, since not all girls like being struck,
think twice before you use the loveblows.

---

3. Burton believed these were iron instruments, but it is quite
clear that they were certain formations of the fist and fingers,
perhaps derived from dance-gestures. See p. 102, note 5.
Yashodhara describes them in detail.

The couple are leaning back in a posture that somewhat resembles the *Yugmapada* of *Ratirahasya*, and he appears to be striking her in the *Samatala* way. Yashodhara expands upon Vatsyayana's remarks about the more dangerous blows, confiding that Shatkarni was so filled with desire at the sight of Malyavati who, after a long illness, had dressed in her best clothes for a festival, that he forgot her fragile condition and struck her during lovemaking. *Pahari, Sikh School, mid nineteenth century*

ORAL PLEASURES

The sages have condemned oral pleasure,
saying it's uncivilized
and strictly forbidden by the *shastras*[1].
Men catch filthy diseases, they say, by kissing
women and eunuchs who have fellated them.

But Vatsyayana says the *shastras*
can neither be applied in the case of eunuchs
(oral sex is their livelihood),
nor in countries whose customs differ from ours.
As for disease, it's easily avoided.

Besides, the *shastras* say four mouths are pure:
the mouth of a suckling calf,
the mouth of a hunting dog seizing its quarry,
the bird's beak severing fruit from trees,
and the mouth of a woman during lovemaking.

But since, in this delicate matter,
the *shastras* seem to contradict one another,
Vatsyayana's advice is that you act
according to your desires, your conscience,
and the customs of your native country.

The eight techniques of fellatio
are normally practised in the following order[2]:
Nimitta (Touching),
Parshvatoddashta (Biting at the Sides),
Bahiha-samdansha (the Outer Pincers).

Antaha-samdansha (the Inner Pincers),
Chumbitaka (Kissing),
Parimrshtaka (Striking at the Tip),
Amrachushita (Sucking a Mango)
and *Sangara* (Swallowed Whole).

When your lover catches your penis
in her hand and, shaping
her lips to an 'O', lays them lightly to its tip,
moving her head in tiny circles,
this first step is called *Nimitta* (Touching).

Next, grasping its head in her hand,
she clamps her lips tightly about the shaft,
first on one side then the other,
taking great care that her teeth don't hurt you:
this is *Parshvatoddashta* (Biting at the Sides).

Now she takes the head of your penis
gently between her lips,
by turns pressing, kissing it tenderly
and pulling at its soft skin:
this is *Bahiha-samdansha* (the Outer Pincers).

If next she allows the head to slide
completely into her mouth
and presses the shaft firmly between her lips,
holding a moment before pulling away,
it is *Antaha-samdansha* (the Inner Pincers).

When, taking your penis in her hand
and making her lips very round,
she presses fierce kisses along its whole length,
sucking as she would at your lower lip,
it is called *Chumbitaka* (Kissing).

If, while kissing, she lets her tongue
flick all over your penis
and then, pointing it, strikes repeatedly
at the sensitive glans-tip,
it becomes *Parimrshtaka* (Striking at the Tip).

And now, fired by passion, she takes
your penis deep into her mouth,
pulling upon it and sucking as vigorously
as though she were stripping clean a mango-stone:
this is *Amrachushita* (Sucking a Mango).

When she senses that your orgasm
is imminent she swallows up the whole penis,
sucking and working upon it
with lips and tongue until you spend:
this is *Sangara* (Swallowed Whole).

Cunnilingus Techniques – Ratiratnapradipika[3]
Worship at your lady's shrine
with these eight techniques of cunnilingus:
Adhara-sphuritam (the Quivering Kiss),
Jihva-bhramanaka (the Circling Tongue)
and *Jihva-mardita* (the Tongue Massage).

Chushita (Sucked), *Uchchushita* (Sucked Up),
Kshobhaka (Stirring),
Bahuchushita (Sucked Hard) and *Kakila* (the Crow);
improvising a little with your teeth
will bring endless variety to these lovegames.

---

1. In this context, the love texts as well as various *Dharmasutras*.

2. Vatsyayana here describes the appearance, habits and manners of the eunuchs who practised fellatio for a living. I have omitted this section and given the techniques as performed, say, by a man's wife, thus also complementing the excerpt from *Ratiratnapradipika*, which follows.

3. *Ratiratnapradipika* is the only love text which gives a complete list of cunnilingus techniques. See Glossary for note on this and other medieval texts.

Both fellatio and cunnilingus were common themes in the temple sculpture of
Khajuraho. In medieval times oral practices were condemned, but by the time of
Ratiratnapradipika a more liberal view pertained. In this cloth painting the girl,
encouraged by her royal lover's benign gaze, has worked her way through perhaps
half the detailed techniques recommended by Vatsyayana. *Orissa, nineteenth century*

With delicate fingertips,
pinch the arched lips of her house of love
very very slowly together,
and kiss them as though you kissed her lower lip:
this is *Adhara-sphuritam* (the Quivering Kiss).

Now spread, indeed cleave asunder,
that archway with your nose and let your tongue
gently probe her *yoni*,
with your nose, lips and chin slowly circling:
it becomes *Jihva-bhramanaka* (the Circling Tongue).

Let your tongue rest a moment
in the archway to the flower-bowed Lord's temple
before entering to worship vigorously,
causing her seed to flow:
this is *Jihva-mardita* (the Tongue Massage).

Next, fasten your lips to hers
and take deep kisses
from this lovely one, your beloved,
nibbling at her and sucking hard at her clitoris:
this is called *Chushita* (Sucked).

Cup, lift her young buttocks,
let your tongue-tip probe her navel, slither down
to rotate skilfully in the archway
of the love-god's dwelling and lap her love-water:
this is *Uchchushita* (Sucked Up).

Stirring the root of her thighs,
which her own hands
are gripping and holding widely apart,
your fluted tongue drinks at her sacred spring:
this is *Kshobhaka* (Stirring).

Place your darling on a couch,
set her feet to your shoulders, clasp her waist,
suck hard and let your tongue stir
her overflowing love-temple:
this is called *Bahuchushita* (Sucked Hard).

If the pair of you lie side by side,
facing opposite ways,
and kiss each other's secret parts
using the fifteen techniques described above,
it is known as *Kakila* (the Crow).

Concluding Remarks – Kama Sutra
So immensely pleasurable is the Crow[4]
to women that for its sake
many courtesans have deserted respectable,
virtuous citizens and taken up
with slaves, barbers, *mahouts*[5] and other low types.

Women who are locked away in harems
often practise the Crow.
Some debauched citizens practise it in secret
with intimate male friends,
lying side by side fellating one another.

Indeed, many young dandies who affect
earrings and other ornaments
are not averse to fellating their fellow men,
but the prima donnas of the oral arts
are eunuchs, harlots, nursemaids and slave-girls.

Oral intercourse should be avoided
by high-priests, *brahmins*[6], royal ministers,
kings, politicians and anyone
of social standing who values his reputation,
for its ethics are extremely doubtful.

It isn't enough to claim these practices
are not condemned by the *shastras*,
which are stores of advice against all eventualities
and inevitably contain ideas
that, taken out of context, will seem wicked.

In the Ayurvedic medical texts[7]
you will find the statement
that dog's meat is both tasty and nutritious,
but does this honestly mean
that everyone should now start eating dog?

The *shastras* can advise you sensibly
on most sexual questions,
but if you're in doubt, observe the proprieties
of place, time and local custom
and rely, ultimately, on your own conscience.

Since all these things are done in private
and kept deadly secret,
and as passion will always overpower reason,
who can say what anyone will do,
or why, or how, or where, when and with whom?

---

4. In *Historia Naturalis* (X: 32) Pliny the Elder pours scorn on the Greek belief that ravens, which they invoked at weddings, mated and laid their eggs through their beaks. He quotes an old wives' tale that pregnant women should avoid ravens' eggs lest they give birth through their mouths. In Juvenal (II: 63) and Martial (XIV: 74) we find that the Romans called men who indulged in cunnilingus 'crows'.

5. Elephant drivers

6. The priestly caste

---

7. The medical texts of Caraka (first or second century AD) and Sushruta (fourth century AD) bear some resemblance to the systems of Hippocrates and Galen, but in other respects were more advanced. In essence their system, which like medieval European medicine was based on a system of humours (*dosha*), is still preserved in the homoeopathic system of modern India. Fa Hsien, in the early fifth century, recorded that free hospitals existed for the poor, maintained by donations from the well-to-do. Ancient Indian doctors were especially skilled in surgery (the caesarian section was known), bone-setting and plastic surgery (the repair of noses, ears and lips mutilated in battle).

Any pleasure great enough to make a courtesan forsake a
wealthy lover for a pauper must, as Vatsyayana knew well,
have been exquisite indeed. Here, perhaps using the complete
armoury of techniques supplied by *Ratiratnapradipika*, a pair of
royal lovers, naked save for their sumptuous jewelry, enjoy
Kakila, the Crow. The intricacy and delicacy of the painting echo
the sensations of the couple, and the painter has caught the
tenderness and compassion of their lovemaking. *Bundi, late
eighteenth century*

HOW TO BEGIN AND END LOVEMAKING

In your drawing room, lit
by the glow of soft incenses,
sit quietly,
garlanded in pale jasmine,
and await your lover's arrival.

When, freshly bathed with anklets jingling,
she comes at last,
walking loose-hipped among her servants,
go out to meet her with a cup
of honey-scented wine.

Put your arm around her shoulders,
teasing her if she's shy,
and while she's laughing at some shameless
piece of gossip you've been saving,
seat her firmly beside you on the cushions.

Begin a light-hearted conversation,
touching at first only her hands and hair,
but steer the talk
and your restless fingers
into discussing ever more delicate questions.

As the lutes of your musicians
slowly awaken her desire,
you should praise the beauty of the dancers,
talking of Art, but leaving her
in some doubt as to which art you mean.

Give her your jasmine for the dance-girls,
then lie her gently back
and, pressing a *paan*[1] between her lips
and making sure her cup is kept well filled,
massage her body with sweet sandal-oil.

Soon she won't object
to fingers that stray under her skirt-hem
and linger at her lightly-knotted waistband;
when her eyes are dreamy and her
breathing's harsh send the servants away.

Now, with her lips parted for passionate kisses,
her hair dishevelled
and her skirt, which you should now gently untie,
riding up her thighs,
your lady is ready for love.

After the lovemaking is over
she may avoid your eyes
and act as though that abandoned creature,
whose body crushed those petals
on the bed, had been a different woman.

But, after you've both washed
and you've salved her bruises with sandal-oil
and cuddled her and given her your cup
to drink from and made a fuss of her,
this shyness will soon vanish.

When she asks for water, as she will,
let your servants appear again,
bringing trays of juice –
mango, lemon, sweet lime –
and a feast of light, delicious snacks.

Consommé to revive her strength[2],
kebabs, crisp vegetables,
candied oranges, nut-studded *halvas*[3],
sherbets and liqueurs
and any other foods you know she likes.

Then, making yourselves comfortable
upon rugs and cushions
spread out on the terrace
in the moonlight,
you may quietly enjoy each other's company.

Let her lie in your lap
with her face turned up to the moon;
point out Polaris and the Morning Star,
the Great Bear and his seven *rishis*[4],
and tell her all the stories of the night sky.

1. See p. 28, note 3

2. Damodara Gupta recommends mutton broth to exhausted
prostitutes in *Kuttani Mata* (V: 307).

3. A family of sweets that range from a sort of Turkish delight
to honeyed fruit and vegetable purees. Carrot *halva* is a great
favourite in modern India.

4. The seven stars of the Great Bear. See Glossary.

एजा्बसनगिर्श

Fanned by attentive servant-girls, the gentleman lovingly
embraces his lady and offers her a *paan*. The painting is one of a
set which illustrates the *Rasikapriya* of the poet Keshavdas.
Malwa, central India, c.1680

LOVERS' QUARRELS

The surest way to provoke a girl
who loves you is to talk,
while you're making love with her,
about your old sweetheart,
or to call her at orgasm by the other girl's name.

This will start a violent row.
Tossing her head in rage,
weeping stormily, her long hair flying loose
in gales of hysterical abuse,
she will beat on your chest with small fists.

If you have been superbly tactless,
she will wrench the flowers
from her neck, trample them,
fling down the treasured ornaments you gave her
before she too falls weeping to the floor.

You must now try to console her,
choosing your words with care
and even, if it is absolutely necessary,
kneeling at her feet, begging her
to forgive you and come back to bed.

But do not be surprised
if your loving words fetch screams of anger
or if, catching hold of your hair
and twisting your face towards her,
she kicks you furiously about the body and head.

Now, hastily pulling on her skirt
and tying the waist with trembling fingers,
dashing aside the great tears
that will not stop welling in her eyes,
she goes off in dudgeon to sulk in the doorway.

If she has read her Dattaka[1]
she will remember his advice that, no matter
how angry she may feel at this point,
she should not leave the room:
how, after all, could she return with dignity?

She sits sobbing in the doorway
and will not budge until you humble yourself
with contrition and promises,
when, caustically accepting your homage,
she smiles through her tears and lets you hug her.

If you quarrel with a wife
and she storms away to her room,
you may be sure she'll be back before long,
angrier than before,
and the whole business will begin again.

But if your lover has gone home,
lose no time in sending your *pithamardas*[2],
vitas and *vidushakas* to pacify her.
She will gradually relent and allow herself
to be led back to your bed for the night.

Concluding Remarks
This ends the book of Lovemaking.
If you are expert
in Babhravya's sixty-four Panchalite arts
and study *Kama Sutra*,
you will never have difficulty with women.

But, no matter how skilled you are
in other sciences, you cannot,
if ignorant of these arts, command respect
among the wise, nor complete
the triple quest for *Dharma*, *Artha* and *Kama*[3].

Indeed, you can be ignorant of all
save these sixty-four arts
and yet win respect in sophisticated circles.
Speak well on this subject and you'll
soon be *guru* to dozens of society men and women.

The old sages praised these arts
because they so greatly strengthened marriage;
the guilds of courtesans
worship the very name of Babhravya,
and which of us dare contradict their authority?

These arts are the most beautiful ways
we know to express love
and, like the women who adore them,
their beauty is both earthly and divine –
so wrote the sages in the *shastras*[4].

---

1. See Glossary. This piece of advice comes from Dattaka's
lectures to the courtesans of Pataliputra.

2. See p. 32, note 14

3. See p. 18, note 1, and Introduction

4. Sacred texts

This vignette, from a rare manuscript of *Amarushataka*, a poem
which records the amorous exploits of the poet-king Amaru,
shows the final stage of a lovers' quarrel. Amaru has
unwittingly called his lover by another girl's name, provoking
the reaction Vatsyayana foretold, and he now says,
disarmingly, that if she's determined to quarrel she must give
him back all the kisses and embraces he has given her. *Malwa,
c.1680*

BOOK III
COURTSHIP

CHOOSING A BRIDE

The aims of marriage, which are
to fulfil *Dharma*, to create wealth and heirs,
and to enjoy love and sexual pleasure,
can only be achieved by marrying a virgin
of your own caste in a proper *Vedic*[1] ceremony.

Choose a girl of good breeding
at least three years younger than yourself.
Her parents, who must still be living,
should have brought her up strictly,
and she should have several uncles and aunts.

Her family should be wealthy,
well respected, with friends in high places
and an impeccable history.
Her relatives and kinsmen should be connected
with the best families in the land.

Your prospective bride should be beautiful,
well behaved, charming and healthy,
with good teeth, nails, ears, hair, eyes and breasts,
and a body entirely free of blemishes.
You, naturally, must be no less of a catch.

It is the sacred duty of your parents
and relatives to find you a suitable bride
and, when they have picked a girl,
to do everything in their power
to win her parents' consent to the marriage.

They should acquaint her parents
with the appalling habits of the other suitors,
warning of trouble in the future,
but praise your pedigree, courage and character,
saying whatever they think will please her mother.

Go to her house disguised as
an astrologer and tell her mother confidently
that her daughter's horoscope,
confirmed by omens like the cawing of crows,
predicts nothing but prosperity for the marriage.

Tell her mother also that the stars
are set against the suitor of her choice –
the match would be a disaster –
and she'd do much better to marry her daughter
to the young man you recommend.

The families should now compare horoscopes,
question the augurs and the *Veda*[2],
go early to a neighbour's house to hear the oracle[3],
and thus fix a suitable wedding day,
avoiding the sixth and eighth days of the month.

Ghotakamukha says the wedding
should not be arranged
solely between the two sets of parents,
but that relatives and friends on both sides
should be allowed to have their say.

Check carefully that the girl
is not lazy, neurotic
or wayward, that she has no secret lover,
nor a reputation for loose living,
and be sure her hair's her own and not a wig.

Reject girls who look like men,
who are scarred by smallpox,
whose hands and feet sweat in the summer,
who stoop or are dumb or are
cursed with disgracefully large backsides.

You may not marry a girl
named inauspiciously after a star, river or tree,
nor one whose name ends in '*la*' or '*ra*',
nor a girl who is too young for you,
nor a friend with whom you played as a child.

Your Daughter's Wedding
When your daughter comes of age
and you judge it is time to find her a husband,
make sure she is elegantly dressed
whenever she leaves the house,
and start to think about her *varana*[4] ceremonies.

Take every opportunity to show her off
at sacrifices, weddings, parties and festivals.
Just as an object for sale needs displaying,
society must notice your daughter's beauty
before it will start to think of her for its sons.

When a suitor whom your wife judges
sufficiently handsome, gifted and eloquent
arrives with his family for the *varana*,
you should welcome them ceremoniously
and offer them the auspicious curds and rice.

---

1. Taken from the *Vedas*, for which see Glossary.

2. See Glossary

3. A person who needed an omen would go, in the small hours, to a neighbour's house and eavesdrop outside, listening for the first word spoken. A pleasant word meant a favourable answer to the petitioner's question. A surly or quarrelsome word portended disaster.

4. The ceremonial meeting of the prospective in-laws, during which the bride-to-be would be on show and would, discreetly, be put through her paces.

A young girl with her pet fawn, in a Golconda garden.
Golconda was the almost legendary kingdom from where the
Koh-i-Noor diamond came, and the girl is possibly a daughter
of one of the courtiers of its last king, Sultan Abul Hasan, for
the picture was painted only some seven years before the fall of
the city to Aurangzeb. The bold use of colour is characteristic of
the Golconda school of painting which, after the Mughal
conquest, moved to nearby Hyderabad. *Golconda, c.1680*

Allow them a fleeting glimpse
of the girl, who may enter to serve snacks
and who, by some extraordinary chance,
is dressed in her finest clothes
and decked out in all the family jewels.

Do not promise his family anything
until you're convinced the young man is suitable.
State merely that you will consult
your relatives and friends
and give them your decision within a few days.

Should his party express a wish to bathe
and eat the ritual meal with you that very day,
you must warn them against haste,
saying that things will take care of themselves
in good time, if Prajapati so wills it.

If you decide in the young man's favour,
plan your daughter's wedding,
according to your national and family traditions,
choosing between the *Brahma*, *Prajapatya*,
Arsha and *Daiva*[5] ceremonies sanctified by the *Veda*.

One should mix, make friends and marry
strictly within one's own caste.
Marry above you and her relations will treat you
little better than a servant,
beneath you and you'll tyrannize her family.

Such marriages are to be avoided.
The couple who marry within their own caste,
sharing friends and interests,
make an alliance of true equals:
the only kind of marriage worth considering.

---

5. The four forms of marriage considered completely
respectable. *Brahma* is giving the girl freely to a suitable man.
Prajapatya is allowing the girl to marry a suitable man of her
own choice. *Daiva* is giving the girl freely to a sacrificial priest of
the *Rig Veda*. In the *Arsha* or *Rishi* form, a gift of two oxen is
made to the girl's father.

A young man arrives to pay a social call on a girl's family. The girl and her friend have seen him coming and hold a hurried discussion. The painting was made to illustrate the *Rasikapriya* and is one of a set now scattered across the world. It owes the main features of its style to the artist Sahibdin, who had painted an influential *ragamala* (personifications of various *ragas*) some twenty years earlier. *Mewar, c.1650 (detail)*

WINNING HER CONFIDENCE

For three nights after the wedding
you must sleep on the floor
and observe a vow of strict celibacy.
Your food should be bland,
entirely free of spices, sugar and salt.

Let your house, for seven days and nights,
be filled with singing;
set musicians behind carved screens
to play as you bathe together,
and dress only in your finest clothes and jewels.

Send flowers and perfumes to your families,
and seat your bride beside you
at every meal, at parties and at the theatre.
These customs hold for all castes:
brahmins, kshatriyas, vaishyas and shudras[1].

On each of the three nights of celibacy,
bid them light your shy wife
to the bridal chamber where, wooing her
with great compassion, you must
painstakingly earn her trust and affection.

Babhravya warns that if you behave,
during these first nights,
with the chaste decorum of a carved stone pillar,
showing no desire at all, your bride may
wonder miserably if she has married a eunuch.

It is a ticklish business, this wooing.
You must kiss and caress her,
gradually building her confidence and desire.
But neither break your celibacy
nor force attentions upon her against her will.

Women are delicate as flowers and need
to be handled as carefully.
If you are rough, or inconsiderate,
she will start hating sex,
but earn her trust and you'll soon win her love.

When she can relax in your presence,
reach out and touch her body
very gently, where it cannot cause any offence.
Stroke her lovingly, but casually,
and never let these caresses last too long.

If you were strangers until the wedding,
confine your caresses
to her breasts and the upper half of her body;
resist the temptation to send your fingers
on exploratory sorties below her navel.

If you've known each other for some time,
she will scarcely demand that you
extinguish the oil-lamps before you embrace her,
but if she's shy, or very young,
allow her modesty to gown itself with darkness.

When she softens under the onslaught
of your expert fingers,
fold a scroll of sweet paan[2], place it
between your lips,
and invite her to capture it with her own.

Plead with her, if she refuses.
Say her shyness is absurd; promise her a jewel.
Finally, fall to your knees and beg:
no woman, however shy or angry,
can ever bear to see her husband at her feet.

When at last she takes the paan,
kiss her softly, wordlessly, upon the mouth.
And if this seems to please her,
begin a more intimate conversation, teasing her
with innocently phrased questions.

Naturally, she will not answer,
and you will have to repeat your question,
patiently urging her to speak.
If still she won't reply, control your temper,
and don't press her any further.

Ghotakamukha says that although
a newly-married bride is often too shy to speak,
or else stammers in terrified confusion,
she treasures every word her husband says,
and misses nothing of his manner.

Questions like 'Do you find me attractive?',
'Do you want me?', will elicit
long, fraught silences before at last she may,
perhaps, favour you with a nod;
but you may very well wait all night for an answer.

Ask her best friend to help you thaw her.
Sitting between you at dinner,
the other girl should encourage you
in your protestations of love, egging you on
to more and more fantastic speeches.

Your wife, at this, will lower her eyes
and break into giggles,
recovering herself sufficiently to round on
her friend and scold her, asking
how she dares be a party to such nonsense.

---

1. See p. 22, note 5
2. See p. 28, note 3

The shy young bride is led to the bedchamber where her husband awaits. A favourite theme in Kangra painting, in this case it is tied in with the legend of Radha and Krishna. Although their love was sung by poets like Jayadeva in his lyrical masterpiece *Gita Govinda*, Radha was actually married to someone else. In this poignant painting, therefore, she is led not to Krishna but to her new husband, while Krishna watches from a distant window. *Kangra, c.1820*

Her friend, undaunted, should flatter you
with a string of confidences
which she claims to have had from your wife,
to whom she now turns, saying:
'Your husband asks why you're so silent now'.

Your wife replies, in a very small voice:
'I didn't say those things.
And if you're going to tease me, I shan't speak.'
But she smiles faintly to herself,
and glances at you from the corners of her eyes.

You will know that these gentle ploys
are working on her feelings
when, one morning, she appears bringing *paan*,
sandalwood-paste and flowers,
and lays them silently at your feet.

Catch her hand, then, and let your nails
rake lightly across her nipples;
refuse to stop, when she objects, and tell her:
'I shall need a great big hug
before I can even consider letting you go'.

Take her on to your lap and let your hand
ride south from her belly-button.
Stop, if she objects again, and swear
the hand will go no further:
this promise doesn't bind your other hand.

Frighten her, if she wriggles,
by saying 'I'll leave lovebites on your lips
and breasts, cover my own body
with nailmarks and tell your friends
you made them. What will you say then?'

Thus coercing your innocent bride
with threats that would scarcely fool a child,
you should, by the third night,
have initiated her into the lesser love-mysteries
and be preparing her for final union.

Cover her body in kisses, and caress
her thighs, your hand slowly
working her skirt up higher and higher.
If she stops you, ask: 'What harm is it doing?',
but pause before renewing the assault.

When she is too aroused to protest,
gently unfasten her girdle,
and loosen the knot of her skirt sufficiently
to slide your fingers down between
her naked thighs and explore her secret places.

By now, your vow of celibacy will be poised
on the edge of ruin, but remember
that these acts are not for your pleasure, but hers:
to awaken her love and confidence
and to prepare her lovingly for the marriage-bed.

During these first three nights, describe
the sixty-four lovemaking arts,
speak of how deeply you love her, and tell her
how, intoxicated with desire,
you schemed and plotted to win her love.

Promise her then that you will never,
in all your life, do a single thing to hurt her;
assure her that she need never fear
the jealousy of co-wives,
for while she lives you will never marry again.

If, in this way, you test her feelings,
win her trust, and snare her
in the hunting-net of your affection,
she will, from the start,
be a faithful and loving life-companion.

Neither bow to her every whim and protest,
nor utterly disregard them;
the middle path is the only path to her love:
show her respect, give her pleasure,
win her confidence, and she will love you always.

If, out of compassion for her feelings,
you make no advances at all,
she will consider you as witless as an animal,
rustic beyond redemption,
incapable of understanding how her mind works.

If, on the other hand, you take no trouble
to woo her, but trample her feelings
in a blundering rush to gratify your desire,
you will arouse only fear and anger,
which will woo each other and breed cold hatred.

If your new bride finds no sign of love in you,
she is filled with a bitterness
which time will turn to enmity, open rebellion
and revulsion for sex; you force her
to search for love in the beds of other men[3].

---

3. According to an old verse quoted by Manu (VIII: 37) and Vasishta (XIX: 44), the guilt of the adultress falls upon her husband, who should have made her transgression impossible. The idea is also found in *Mahabharata*, in the story of Ahalya (see Glossary). If the husband goes off to other women the wife does not deserve any blame for breaking faith with him. Women are what men make them.

An amorous married couple snuggle up together against the cold of their Garhwal home. She offers him *paan*, just as she would have had they been living in Vatsyayana's day. The sandalwood paste, too, that the young bride of *Kama Sutra* lays at her husband's feet was much favoured in Garhwal. The state lay spread out along the foothills of what are now the Rishikesh and Chamba Himalayas. The style of painting is almost indistinguishable from the Kangra and Guler styles. *Garhwal, c.1780–1800*

COURTING GAMES

If you suspect that her parents
may refuse their consent to your engagement,
you must woo the girl secretly,
persuade her to elope with you,
and marry her according to the *Gandharva*[1] rite.

If she's very young, almost a child,
you may take her picking flowers,
and weave them for her into long garlands;
give her a doll's house and dolls,
and help her feast them on mud pies and *laddus*[2].

Play all the popular village games,
like tossing up the six pebbles and catching them
deftly on the back of the hand,
blind-man's-buff, hopscotch, tag, hide-and-seek,
and running with arms stretched out like wings.

Hide small coins in heaps of wheat
and say she may keep them if she can find them.
When she is playing with her friends,
make her close her eyes and guess
whose finger is tapping gently upon her forehead.

Weave her a sash from wools and yarns,
grasp her hands and whirl her round and round,
hide your middle finger among the others
and challenge her to pick it out,
or defy her to guess what is hidden in your fist

If she sees something she admires,
buy it for her on the spot,
and bring her toys no other girls possess,
things so rare and exciting
that she can scarcely believe her eyes.

Give her a coloured ball
painted in slices like segments of an orange,
and show her how the colours spin
and blur to white; teach her to float
soap-bubbles from a tiny glass-blowing iron.

Delight her with baby dolls, carved
from wood, horn or ivory,
whose faces, carefully modelled in wax or clay
and fringed with silken hair,
are wreathed in sweet, life-like smiles.

Give her models, each skilfully carved
from a single block of wood, of rams and bulls
yoked in pairs, a couple arm-in-arm,
and a miniature temple, whose painted doors
can be opened and unfolded to the four quarters[3].

Give her cages of parrots, mynahs,
quails, cocks and partridges;
unflawed beautiful conches, butterfly-shells,
cowries and mother-of-pearl;
consecrated amulets and a toy *vina*[4].

Give her a paintbox stocked with lac,
red ochre, yellow orpiment and other pigments;
silver pots of sandalwood-paste,
cardamoms, betel nuts and *paan*[5] leaves;
phials of fragrant attars[6] and other cosmetics.

Make her feel that you'll always
give her everything she wants.
If she asks why you give these gifts secretly,
say you fear her parents
and you don't want her friends to become jealous

Ask her for a secret tryst,
saying you have something important to tell her,
and woo her with romantic tales about girls
like Shakuntala and Damayanti[7], who chose
their own husbands and married for love.

Win over her maid or her nurse's daughter
with flattery, small gifts and kindnesses,
and let her confirm these stories.
This girl's help will be vital to you
whether or not you take her into your confidence.

---

1. The love marriage is when a couple elope, exchange vows before the sacred fire and then immediately consummate their marriage. It cannot be set aside. This chapter, and the two following, are addressed to young men and women who, for whatever reason, cannot marry according to the first four forms (see p.96, note 5). The games of this chapter, the tricks and stratagems of the next and the marriage preparations of the last are all directed towards the Gandharva rite.

2. Round sweetmeats, made with sugar and various kinds of flour or lentils, flavoured with coconut, lime, cashews, cardamoms, almonds, pistachios, raisins, melon seeds and so on.

3. In Rajasthan, small wooden temples painted with scenes from *Ramayana* and the life of Krishna are taken round the villages by wandering *brahmins* who relate the stories before performing *puja*. Double-folding doors open to reveal an inner sanctum which contains the images of Rama, Sita and Laxmana. These temples are very likely the direct descendants of the one Vatsyayana is describing.

4. See p. 28, note 4

5. In almost every Indian household there is a tin or moist cloth containing a stack of fresh leaves for making *paan*. Vatsyayana's *paan* casket would have been a much more ornate affair. In ancient times princes and aristocrats had their own *paan* butlers and the giving and receiving of *paan* was an art. Prince Samarabhata is said (*Kuttani Mata* V: 759) to have taken *paan* with his left hand held in the *Khatakamukha* (Crowbeak?) dance gesture from the *paan* butler's hand, which was in the *Samdansha* (Pincers) posture.

6. Then, as now, sandalwood essence was precious, although today it shares a place with patchouli. Rose attars were unknown in ancient India and are a legacy of the Muslim conquest.

7. See Glossary

A young man offers a box which might contain *paans* or
sweetmeats or which might be a gaming box to a girl whose
favour he wants to win. The girl's maid who, according to *Kama
Sutra* and time-honoured tradition, will be in league with the
suitor, is urging her to accept the gift. *Sirchi, late seventeenth
century*

If your bride-to-be loves magic,
dumbfound her with conjuring and illusions.
If she's fond of music and the arts,
charm her with love-songs;
demonstrate your sensitivity and skills.

On the eighth night of the waning moon
and at other religious festivals,
take to her house fragrant flower-crowns,
a blue lotus to place behind her ear,
seals, rings and richly embroidered clothes.

But be careful to time your arrival
and present these gifts in such a manner
that your actions can neither
by misunderstood, nor spawn
gossip that could destroy your reputation.

Tutor her maid to say
she hears you are very skilled in the arts of love –
far more so than the other young men –
and that any girl who married you would gain
not merely a husband, but an exquisite lover.

The maid should question you,
in the girl's presence, about the sixty-four arts,
enabling you to display your knowledge,
excite her curiosity and begin,
indirectly, to instruct her in the *Kama Sutra*.

Arrange for your beloved
to be forever catching sight of you, and always
dress immaculately before you meet her.
You may judge whether your suit is successful
by the way she acts in your presence.

A girl who loves you will never
look at you directly,
but is always glancing shyly at you
from the corners of her eyes –
she will look at you only when you look away.

Feigning utter nonchalance,
she rearranges the folds of her skirt
to cover herself more modestly,
and carefully displays
much more than she should of her beautiful limbs.

If you ask her something, she smiles,
hangs her head and lisps
some unintelligible reply in broken language.
But she will sit happily
for hours by your side without speaking.

When she sees you in the distance
she stops on some pretext
and asks, making a moue at her maids,
'Do you think he's seen me?' –
of course, she soon makes certain that you have.

Staring in your direction,
she laughs out loud at something she has noticed,
and chatters animatedly,
but in distracted fashion, to her maids,
inventing excuses for not moving on.

She may seize a passing child
and, to its horror, begin to kiss and caress it,
or find something wrong
with the way her forehead-pearls are hanging
and stop to have her maids adjust them.

Surrounded by her girls,
she yawns coquettishly and stretches her limbs,
her whole body speaking her desire;
or she may imitate the way
you stroke your beard and twirl your moustache.

She cultivates your friends
and is generous to your servants, with whom
she plays chess and cards,
treating them as though she were their mistress
and listening for any mention of your name.

She will be persuaded by her maid
to put on her finest clothes and ornaments
and come to your house to sit,
playing chess and dice
and making cheerful conversation.

If you ask her for her ear-flower,
her ring or her garland, she will hesitate,
but will not refuse your request;
she is scarcely ever seen, other than
in the clothes and jewels you have given her.

When you hear that she frowns
and grows gloomy if her mother ever mentions
other suitors, and that she no longer
even mixes with their friends,
you will know that you have won her.

The suitor surprises his beloved with a flower bow like that carried by Kama, the god of love. Kama's bow, however, is made of sugarcane and strung with humming bees. His arrows, like the one in the painting, are tipped with lotuses and have the same deadly effect as Cupid's. To aim such a weapon at a young woman is a clear statement of intent – little wonder she's looking apprehensive. Bilaspur is another of the north Punjab hill states. *Bilaspur, c.1750*

COURTING TRICKS AND STRATAGEMS

When you're certain that the girl
is deeply in love with you,
you must turn her childish adoration to a passion
so blinding that she'll agree both
to sleep with you and to marry you secretly.

Whilst playing chess with her,
dispute one of her moves,
catching her hand as if to prevent an illegality,
but holding it a little too long,
making her aware of a new, deeper intimacy.

When you're walking together,
let your body constantly be touching hers,
and ask, laughing, if it's possible
that your bodies are conspiring to instruct you
in the first four embraces of *Kama Sutra*.

Suggest your desire by showing her
pictures you have found, cut into *bhurja*[1] leaves
and painted in palm-leaf books,
of men and women in erotic postures
and pairs of birds and animals making love.

When you go swimming with her,
wait until she's almost out of her depth,
then swim towards her underwater,
grab her legs and caress her playfully
before surfacing, with a laugh, at her side.

Upon a large, fresh leaf imprint
with your nails, a letter
describing the anguish she is causing you
and fill it with fine phrases, like:
'I dare not think, lest thoughts of you torment me.'

Fasten upon any excuse to speak of how
she haunts you in erotic dreams:
'That skirt! But only last night you came to me
exactly as you are now. I'm dreaming,
I told myself – ah, but was it really just a dream?'

Sit close to her at the theatre
and at clan gatherings,
and, taking great care that no-one sees you,
nudge her conspiratorially
and gently stroke her foot with yours.

Capture her toes between yours,
let your toe-nails scrape lightly across her sole
and, if she doesn't whisper
for you to stop, let your toes slowly
haul themselves towards her thighs and buttocks.

Get her used to small intimacies:
whenever she washes your feet,
trap and squeeze her fingers between your toes;
if she offers you flowers or an orange,
let her palm feel your nails as you accept.

When she pours water for you
to rinse your mouth out after a meal,
smile through your teeth
and soak her with an accurate jet of spray,
laughing as she leaps back in protest[2].

When you're sitting or lying together
on a *charpay*[3] in the dark,
explore her body, tentatively at first
and, if she does not object,
cover her limbs in lightly-printed nailmarks.

Say you have something to tell her.
'What is it?' she will ask;
but let your message of love be conveyed
by gestures, caresses, sighs,
even silence: in fact, by anything but words.

If you wish to test her love,
feign illness and summon her to your bedside.
Ask feebly if she'll massage your head,
saying: 'Only beauty cures pain,
and there is no beauty in the world like you.'

When she is rubbing your temples,
catch hold of her hands
and lay them upon your eyes and forehead,
saying: 'You see? It's fading.
Your hands have more healing than any drug.'

Delay her, when she says it's time
she left, with talk of literature and art.
If you can keep up this shamming
for three days and nights,
you need have no further doubt about her feelings.

Let your conversations revolve
mainly upon the arts and inconsequential gossip.
State love, but not desire, openly:
it is important to convince her
that you are sincere, not merely goaded by lust.

Persevere, for as Ghotakamukha has said,
no matter how fervently
she loves you, nor how deeply she trusts you,
you will never get her into bed
without a great deal of trouble and talk.

---

1. See p. 24, note 5

2. The touch of another's mouth is thought to pollute food and
drink, therefore this act would imply great intimacy.

3. A wooden or bamboo bed, strung with coir fibre.

The mischievous god Krishna has stolen the clothes of the *gopis*, or milkmaids, while they are bathing in the river Yamuna. He is indifferent to their anger, shame and pleas for mercy, and refuses to return the bright *saris* that festoon the tree in which he is sitting until each of them has emerged, naked, from the water and given him a kiss. This is a favourite theme in Indian painting, and perhaps the story was at the back of Vatsyayana's mind when he advised his reader to take his girlfriend out swimming. *Sholapur Deccani, late eighteenth century*

Only after courting her patiently
and repeatedly testing her love
dare you make preparations for the wedding:
not unless it is her own free choice
can you marry her according to the *Gandharva*⁴ rite.

When evening blues into night
and darkness bolts a door on the world,
desire stirs in young women
and they find it hard to refuse a lover:
it is then that you should ask her to marry you.

So much the better if your proposal
coincides with a sacrifice, wedding or festival,
a long journey or a period of hardship:
at these times people's emotions are in turmoil
and she will be very likely to consent.

In Vatsyayana's opinion, any girl
whose words and actions have already implied
that she's willing to elope, will,
if faced with an impeccably-timed proposal,
find it impossible to recant.

How a Girl Can Snare a Husband
If you are a beauty, but low-born,
of aristocratic stock, but poor or orphaned,
it will be quite impossible
to find a husband in the normal way,
so you will have to arrange your own marriage.

Choose a handsome, capable young man:
one who knew you as a child
or one who is headstrong and impulsive enough
to marry you despite his parents' wishes –
either type should prove easy for you to snare.

Flaunt your charms at him
and attract him with every trick you know;
your mother, if she is living,
and all your friends and servants
should be drafted in to help with your campaign.

Go to meet him in a quiet spot,
taking with you flowers, *paan*⁵ and perfumes
with which to massage his head;
converse with him on his pet subjects,
displaying your knowledge of the sixty-four arts.

But no matter how deeply you desire it,
never ever initiate loveplay.
The sages have said that nothing will destroy
your charm or ruin your chances
faster than seeming too eager for bed.

Conversely, you should accept
and even encourage his amorous advances.
But take care not to allow yourself
to be overwhelmed by his kisses and caresses.
And feign ignorance of his intentions.

When he tilts your chin for a kiss,
resist, and act as though he's forcing you.
If he presses your hand to his penis,
recoil in horror, but, after much argument,
allow yourself to be persuaded just to touch it.

No matter how desperately he begs,
never take your clothes off,
nor permit him the slightest glimpse
of your thighs or secret parts:
what guarantee have you that he'll marry you?

Only when you're quite convinced
that he loves you far too much to let you go,
should you let him end your virginity;
even then be careful quickly
to tell your close friends what has happened⁶.

In this way you cannot fail to win
a worthy, loving husband.
If your prize is capable, attractive
and also madly in love,
do not lose the opportunity to marry him.

If he is poor and undistinguished,
but loves you faithfully
and will always keep you fed and clothed,
consider him very seriously;
but reject men who will marry only your body.

The houses of the wealthy are filled
with spiteful women,
beauties whose richly ornamented facades
should speak of happiness,
but betray only the neglect and ruin within.

Do not marry a man of lower caste,
an old man or a gambler,
a man who travels abroad, a man whose home
is full of other women's children,
or a man who would force you against your will.

If you're only after money,
ignore his ugliness, wives and other women;
but if you're lucky enough to have
a choice of eligible bachelors,
always choose the one who loves you most.

---

4. See p. 102, note 1
5. See p. 28, note 3

6. This, presumably, was so that the man could not easily renege on his promises.

Evening is coming and dark monsoon clouds pile up over the distant hills. One can almost feel the sharpness of the air, cool with the expectation of heavy rain. The last few days before the monsoon are charged with excitement. In the words of the poet Bahadur: 'The restless lightning dances in the dark clouds and young women overcome with passion are seeking their lovers.' What better evening for a proposal? *Garhwal, c.1780–1800*

THE LOVE MARRIAGE

If, because it is difficult
to arrange private meetings with the girl,
you cannot woo her yourself,
bribe her nurse to trumpet your praises
and launch a propaganda war against your rivals.

'My love, such exciting news! Did you know
you have a secret admirer? I haven't met him,
but if half of what they say is true,
he is the husband of your dreams –
oh dear, I've been very foolish to mention this –'

'Pity your parents are so blind – do they think
about compatibility? If you ask me,
all they care about is money, money, money.
They're not considering your happiness –
they'll give you to the first wealthy ape who asks.'

'If only you could choose your own husband
and marry in the old *Gandharva*[1] way –
we love to hear how Shakuntala won Dushyanta[2]
and Subhadra let Arjuna[3] carry her off –
should happy marriages be just for story books?'

'Go ahead, marry money, but mark my words –
your life will be absolute hell.
Think of all his other wives – spiteful women,
causing quarrel after quarrel –
is that really the kind of married life you want?'

'Of course, if daydreams could come true
you'd marry this young man who so adores you
and be his only wife – he's definitely not
the womanizing sort. You wouldn't be wealthy,
but my dear – think how very happy you'd be!'

The nurse should hammer at these ideas
until the girl is swayed,
and then suggest that it could do no harm
to establish tentative contact between you,
and so resolve any remaining doubts.

Playing the skilled go-between, her nurse
should carefully remove the girl's misgivings
and say, to counter her fear of disgrace:
'He'll pretend to carry you off by force.
Nobody will blame you and you'll have won him!'

The Gandharva Wedding

On the night she steals from her father's house,
fetch the sacred fire from a temple,
strew the ground with sweet *kusha*[4] grass
and, offering sacrifice according to the *smritis*[5],
circle the holy fire with her three times.

Once the marriage is consummated
your families are faced with a fait accompli,
for the sages say that marriage vows
made willingly, in the presence
of the sacred fire, can never be revoked.

Quickly then, before the news goes further,
make overtures to her parents who,
terrified of the scandal poised to break
upon their family, will accept you,
however reluctantly, as their son-in-law.

The Asura Marriage[6]

If the girl will not agree to marry you,
it may be possible to buy her.
Offer a large bribe through a friend of her parents
and have her brought, on some pretext,
to your house, where the sacred fire is waiting.

Or, if the girl's parents have already
engaged her to marry someone else,
and the date of her wedding is drawing near,
your helper must malign the other man
to the girl's mother, praising you instead.

Her mother's confidence in the fiancé
should be so utterly destroyed
that, in her desperation to prevent the match,
she agrees to fetch fire herself
and marry you, in secret, to her daughter.

Should the girl have a brother of your age
who is entangled with a courtesan,
you can win his friendship, and his sympathy
for your cause, simply
by helping him with the prodigious expense.

---

1. See p. 102, note 5

2, 3. See Glossary

4. *Poa cynosuroides* A sacred long-stemmed grass used at religious ceremonies. The leaf blades and points are razor-sharp. The oil from this plant is of great commercial value and is used in the manufacture of perfume essences and for perfuming expensive soaps.

5. Sacred texts

6. The word literally means 'enemy of the gods', and is applied to a class of devils who are continually warring with the gods. The original Indian and Iranian Aryans called their gods 'sura'. It is thought that a family tiff resulted in the Iranians renaming their gods 'asura', so that the Indian gods became Iranian devils and vice versa.

An elopement by night. The lover has brought his elephant through a lotus-filled lake to an unguarded part of the palace, where his princess awaits him. Helped by her maids, she slides precariously down a rope as he reaches up to guide her safely into the *howdah*. The subject combines adventure with romance, an irresistible lure to any Mughal painter. *Mughal, late eighteenth century*

He will lure the girl to your house
and marry you in the presence of the sacred fire:
when close friends have been known to
give their lives for one another,
why should such a man refuse to give his sister?

The Paishacha Marriage[7]
During *Ashtmi*[8] or another moonlight festival,
bribe her nurse to get her tipsy
and lead her to some dark, desolate place
where you can have your will with her:
after this, no other man will want to touch her.

Catching a girl when she is drowsy,
or intoxicated by drugs, and deflowering her
before she realizes what is happening
is the evil *Paishacha* form of bride-taking:
do not insult the gods by bringing fire.

The Rakshasa Marriage[9]
If, learning that the girl is on her way
to a garden or a nearby village,
you ride out, heavily armed, and kidnap her,
killing or scattering her guards,
it is the *Rakshasa* form of bride-taking.

So far as *Dharma*[10] is concerned,
the *Gandharva* form of marriage is the best.
Asura is degrading, *Paishacha* evil
and *Rakshasa* is the worst of all,
the last resort of a desperate, foolish man.

Since marriage aims to kindle love,
what could be more fruitless
than to inspire hatred from the start?
Even if you have used a go-between,
the *Gandharva* marriage is far and away the best.

Gandharva is the happy, beautiful marriage,
entered willingly, without fear
or sorrow, born of love freely given and returned –
Gandharva is the love-marriage
and, for this reason, it is the best of all.

---

7. A class of ogres, named either for their corpselike colour
(*pita*=yellow) or because of their craving for flesh (*pisa*=flesh).

8. The eighth night after the full moon.

9. A class of demons hostile to mankind, who haunted
cemeteries and feasted on corpses. Their stronghold was Lanka
(Ceylon) where Ravana, their king, took Sita after her capture,
which led to the war of the *Ramayana*. See also p. 34, note 4.

10. Spiritual and moral duty. See p. 18, note 1, and
Introduction.

Because most Indian marriages were, and still are, arranged, the *Gandharva*, or love marriage, was considered daring and rather romantic, and the bond of love between the couple very precious. It is this that the artist has tried to express in his painting, where an anxious wife directs her maids in preparing the bedroom for her absent husband. One girl arranges the bed while another fetches water and a cloth with which to clean the room. But the lady's thoughts are not on these activities, they are with her lover. *Bilaspur, c.1690–1700*

113

BOOK IV
MARRIAGE

RUNNING THE HOUSEHOLD

If you're his only wife, convince
your husband that in you he has a loyal,
trustworthy companion, whose support
for him will never waver,
and in whose heart he will always reign supreme.

With his permission take over the burden
of managing the household;
remember Gonardiya's[1] remark that nothing
pleases a husband more
than coming home to a clean, orderly house.

Keep the house well swept and dusted,
tidy and always fragrant;
garland doors and archways with marigolds,
and have the courtyard smoothed
over with cool, fresh-scented cowdung[2].

The family shrine must be spotless
and used for worship
three times each day – at dawn, noon and dusk.
Decorate the floor for festivals,
light the lamps, and perform special *pujas*[3].

Should they be living with you,
show the greatest respect
for the older members of your husband's family.
Treat your servants well; this is
the first secret of any efficient household.

In a tidy, pleasant corner of the garden,
plant brakes of sugarcane, and beds
of the herbs and spices the kitchen needs daily:
turmeric, coriander, ginger, spinach, cumin,
mustard-seed, celery, fennel and cinnamon.

Perfume the garden with thickets of flowers
like the moss rose, pearl-jasmine,
Arabian and Spanish jasmines, yellow amaranth,
frangipani[4], night-jasmine[5],
kadamba[6], and looping clusters of the China rose.

Plant flowering groves of Indian coral
and catechu trees, banana palms
and tall stands of fragrant *khus-khus*[7] grass.
Footpaths should lead from the house
and wander between the flowers and trees.

In the middle of this lovely garden
you should sink a deep well,
or a pool with steps leading down to the water,
or a lotus-covered reservoir
beside which you can sit in the summer.

Avoid entanglements with beggar women,
Buddhist or Jain nuns,
harlots, dancing girls, gypsy women, sybils
and pythonesses, and shun
any woman who practises Muladeva's[8] black arts.

Serve your husband with his favourite dishes,
made from pure, wholesome ingredients.
Your kitchen should be clean, well-ventilated,
fully-equipped, and hidden away
where guests and strangers cannot see inside.

When you hear your husband's voice
as he enters the house,
come out into the courtyard and welcome him,
asking yourself what he needs
and what you can do to make him comfortable.

When the servant-girl comes to wash his feet
excuse her gently, saying
that you would like to do it yourself.
Never welcome him, even privately,
without having dressed to look your best.

If your husband is spending too heavily,
or frittering money away,
you should speak to him about it in private.
If he offends you, control your anger,
but ask him, icily, never to do that again.

Scold and reproach him when you're alone,
or sitting with close friends,
but never try to control him by using witchcraft:
Muladeva's arts are the root cause,
says Gonardiya, of mistrust in marriages.

Ask your husband's permission before going
on your own to weddings,
friends' houses, clan-gatherings or temples
and if you want to compete in games
and races at festivals like the Night of the Yakshas[9].

---

1. See Glossary

2. Cowdung is one of the five gifts of the cow. It can be used, packed in dry cakes, as fuel and, mixed with chaff, to plaster walls and floors. It gives a smooth, cool surface and has a scent rather like henna or new-mown hay.

3. Usually an offering of incense, flowers and water, performed in a sacred *mandala* or floor design in the presence of the holy fire.

4. See p. 36, note 7

5. *Tabernaemontana coronaria* Commonly known throughout India as *raat-ki-rani* (Queen of the Night). It is very fragrant at night.

6. See p. 32, note 13

7. See p. 110, note 4

8. See Glossary

9. A religious festival corresponding to modern *diwali*. See p. 30, including note 8, and see also Glossary for Yakshas.

A young wife lovingly tends her garden, preparing it for her absent husband. Every line in her body speaks of the care she is taking, and the plants have responded. Behind her a *Kadamba* tree is blossoming; the banana has a purple flower and is about to fruit; the scarlet creepers seem to be trying to please her. In the foreground a pet peacock is killing a centipede, a touch which leaves us in no doubt as to the lady's efficiency. *Bundi, c.1680*

Avoid bad habits like using foul language,
flirting with your eyes, scowling,
standing at your front door eyeing passers-by,
locking yourself away in your room,
or stealing into the garden to gossip with friends.

Never allow yourself to smell sweaty,
or to let tartar collect in
the crevices of your teeth and cause bad breath;
nothing is more calculated
to arouse revulsion in your husband.

When desire stirs you to visit
your husband's bed, put on your jewelry,
anoint yourself with perfumed oils,
place a flower in your hair,
and go to him wearing bright, clean clothes.

When out for a stroll together,
you should dress in light, filmy silks,
wear necklace and earrings only,
white flowers in your hair,
and the faintest touch of sandalwood perfume.

Demonstrate your love by keeping fasts
and sharing penances with him,
and ask him not to forbid these gestures.
Go to bed only when he is asleep,
and wake before he does without disturbing him.

Haggle over the price of household goods,
buying cheaply and stocking
supplies of clay waterpots, bamboo poles,
wicker baskets and stools,
string-beds, headrests and other wooden items.

Your kitchen should be equipped
with a sturdy iron *tava*[10],
a copper soup-ladle and pair of tongs,
at least one large cauldron,
and a set each of iron, copper and brass pans.

Fill clay pots with rock salt, sea salt,
ghee[11], oil and other essentials,
fragrant pot-pourris of night-jasmine petals
and other flowers used in perfumery,
pumpkin gourds and various bitter flavourings.

Similarly, you should lay in stocks
of herbal medicines and drugs,
and any other commodities which are seasonal
or in short supply,
and hide them in secret places about the house.

Collect seeds of radish, yam, olibanum, mango,
wormwood, cucumber, muskmelon, aubergine,
pumpkin, calabash, parsnip, pomegranate,
cowhage, caravalla, garden-quinine,
garlic and onion, and sow each at the right season.

Keep your financial position a secret,
shared only with your husband;
on no account go telling other people,
especially not strangers,
how much money is hidden away in the house.

You should aim to excel all your peers
in the sixty-four arts and sciences,
to outshine them in dress, manner and bearing,
in your devotion to your husband,
and in your extraordinary talent for haute cuisine.

Prepare your annual budget carefully
and try never to exceed it;
you should know how to economize by churning
ghee from left-over curds,
and how to extract molasses from sugarcane pith.

Learn how to press oil from sesame seeds,
how to spin yarn from cotton bolls
and weave it into bolts of cloth for dressmaking;
collect and pulp strips of bark,
and plait the fibre into ropes and hanging baskets.

Supervise your servant girls as they pound,
winnow and clean rice and wheat.
Save the chaff for mixing with cowdung
and plastering floors and walls,
and the small broken grains for your pet birds.

Keep half-burned coals and sticks of charcoal,
and learn to use them a second time.
Teach your servants to practise economies;
look to their food and welfare,
and concern yourself with the fields and livestock.

---

10. A shallow bowl-shaped cooking pot, similar to the Chinese *wok*, with handles on either side, used for cooking flat breads and also for deep-frying.

11. Clarified butter, considered a great delicacy and still the most expensive fat available in India.

The lady of the house accepts *paan* from a maid as she and her old nurse supervise the servants, who are washing pots and pans and cooking over a clay hearth. Indian homes are ideally built round courtyards and have two hearths, one in the open air. The cook squats in front of the fire, feeding it with twigs, fanning it to maintain the right heat and to dispel the smoke, and using iron tongs to lift pots on and off. Cooking, these days, is usually done in brass pots. Water is stored in clay pots, which keep cool in hot weather. Any shelf above a door may house a row of drying onions or a ripening pumpkin. If the family stores grain, it may be in wooden chests, or clay jars as tall as a man, with heavy wooden lids. *Kangra, c.1790 (detail)*

Take it upon yourself to care for the tame
rams, cocks, quails, parrots,
mynahs, doves, peacocks, monkeys and deer.
And it is your duty as a good wife
to keep a daily tally of income and expenditure.

Have your husband's old clothes washed,
patched, and dyed if necessary,
and give them to servants you wish to reward.
If the clothes are not fit to wear,
tear them up and use them for dusters and wicks.

Keep a close watch on your stocks
of *sura* and *asava*[12] wines,
and superintend their production and use.
You will need a separate ledger
for income and expenditure on wines and spirits.

When your husband's friends come to visit,
welcome them hospitably
with garlands of jasmine from the garden,
dabs of sandalwood perfume,
and fresh *paans*[13] which you have made yourself.

Take good care of your parents-in-law;
always respect their wishes,
and resist the temptation to answer them back.
Lower your voice in their presence,
and conduct yourself with modesty and discretion.

Stifle the impulse to laugh out loud
at their old-fashioned views;
honour their friends as though they were yours,
and don't antagonize them
by seeming too friendly with people they dislike.

Never let it be said of you that possessions
and wealth have made you snobbish,
and always behave with the utmost courtesy
towards members of the family,
tradesmen, servants, labourers and slaves alike.

Keep your servants interested in their work
by allotting each a special duty.
Reward them, at festivals and on feast-days,
with gifts of food and clothing,
after your husband has given his consent.

When your husband is abroad,
wear no jewels except auspicious conch bangles,
offer *pujas* and prayers for his safety,
fast more often than usual,
and send regularly for any news of his return.

At night you should have your bed brought
to the foot of your mother-in-law's;
ask her permission before you begin any penance,
draw on her experience, and obey her
when she forbids you to continue a long fast.

Continue to run the household according
to your husband's parting advice;
spend within your budget, yet maintain
the house and lands efficiently,
and try to complete any works that he had begun.

Carry on with all his business ventures,
filling the treasure-chests,
buying and selling with the help of honest,
faithful servants, and cutting back,
wherever possible, on the household expenses.

Go round the house collecting together
all the silly little things
of which your husband was most fond,
and arrange them lovingly
in your room for safekeeping until his return.

During his absence, visit your parents
only on important occasions
like weddings or funerals; go accompanied by
your husband's men, dress simply,
and do not stay longer than a few days.

When your husband comes home,
let him find you austerely dressed in white
as though mourning his absence;
welcome him with gifts,
and offer a *puja* to celebrate his safe return.

Fulfil your wifely *Dharma*[14] in this way,
and from *Dharma*'s root
Artha will spring and *Kama* will flower;
you will win you husband's love,
and be forever free from the curse of co-wives.

---

12. *Sura* is made from mango-juice and *asava* is flavoured with wood-apples. They were party drinks. See also p. 30.

13. See p. 28, note 3

14. Her duty. *Dharma* comprehends her duty as a Hindu, as a woman and as a wife.

A lady tries to coax her pet monkeys down from the roof, while her servants gather round to offer advice. It would probably be the husband who would have chosen a monkey as a pet, but it would be the duty of the wife to look after it. Monkeys, especially these *langurs* (whom Kipling called the 'bandarlog'), make amusing, intelligent pets and were possibly considered auspicious because of the importance of the monkey-god Hanuman. *Kangra, c.1820 (detail)*

THE POLITICS OF THE HAREM

Lust, a debauched nature, unhappiness,
his wife's inability to produce
sons or any children at all, and sheer imbecility –
these are what drive a man
to marry again while his first wife is still living.

As the first wife you must exercise
devotion, charm and cunning
to deny him any excuse for marrying again;
but if barren it will hurt less
to urge him yourself to take another bride.

Now, it is the tendency of every newlywed
to try and assert her authority
as soon as she possibly can. This will inevitably
cause trouble between you,
and early rivalry can lead to bitter hatred.

You must avoid this by treating the new bride
not as a rival, but like a favourite
little sister, yourself robing and perfuming her
before each evening's lovegames,
and teaching her all you know of the arts of love.

Shrug it off lightly when she jibes at you,
and never allow yourself to brood.
Overlook it when, in your husband's presence,
she makes some gauche mistake –
don't punish her by drawing his attention to it.

But if she seems chastened by her error,
take her aside and explain how
she can avoid it next time; guide her tolerantly
at this stage and you'll convert
a potential enemy into a lifelong friend.

When you begin to instruct the girl
in the arts of lovemaking,
be sure to hold your lessons in a place
where your husband will overhear
you teaching his new bride how to please him.

Treat the children of the second wife
as lovingly as you would if they were yours,
speak courteously to her servants
and do her friends and relatives
even greater honour than you do your own.

The Eldest Wife

If you're the eldest among several wives,
ally yourself to the girl who is next in seniority,
and cause constant quarrels between
your husband's current and former favourites,
secretly assuring each of your support.

If your husband wants to raise his favourite
to the position of senior consort,
you should not act against him yourself,
but set the other wives against her
and see to it that she is utterly crushed.

Keep trouble continually simmering
among the women of the harem:
if a wife falls out with your husband,
deepen their quarrel
by pretending that she has your sympathy.

Should peace threaten the *zenana*[1],
fan the flames industriously,
only stepping forward to end the bickering
when your husband understands
the importance of your role as senior wife.

The Youngest Wife

If you are the youngest wife,
you must regard the eldest as your mother;
never even using the clothes and jewels
your parents and relatives gave you
without first asking and receiving her permission.

Your every duty must be performed
under the supervision of the eldest wife;
you will even have to ask her consent
before you go to your husband's bed,
though both of you know very well it's your turn.

You should appear to love her children
more dearly than your own;
but when you're alone with your husband
you must try to excel her
in charm, wit, devotion and, of course, in bed.

---

1. See p. 28, note 2

The new bride is prepared for a night of love. A maid is busily massaging her feet while the senior wife holds up a mirror. The older wife is asked by Vatsyayana to submerge her own feelings of jealousy and resentment in an attempt to ease the fears of the young girl who, after all, will never know what it is to have a husband to herself. The gaily-striped trousers were the everyday fashion of this region and are also found in Basohli painting, by which this miniature is heavily influenced.

Mankot, c.1730

You must never complain to your husband
of the eldest wife's cruelty
(let the facts be conveyed subtly, by others),
but seize the opportunity, whenever
her back is turned, to corner his affection.

Say to him that you crave his love
more than life itself,
but when you have it do not be so foolish
as to trumpet the fact
or you'll draw the whole harem down upon you.

The woman who flaunts her husband's secrets
has no hope of retaining his trust;
besides, as Gonardiya has sensibly observed,
youngest wives must always be discreet
out of fear of retribution from the senior wives.

In fact, Vatsyayana thinks you should feel pity
for the unhappy, accursed woman
whose infertility has cost her a husband's love,
and demonstrate your sympathy by
urging your husband not to think harshly of her.

The Mistress[2]
A few hedonists will always keep mistresses:
either widows who cannot live
without the joys of a sexual relationship,
or women who have left their husbands for lovers
or because their marriages were unhappy.

Gonardiya says that such a woman,
if she has already walked out on two paramours
because they failed to satisfy her,
will continue to desert lover after lover,
always on the lookout for someone better.

She hops out of one bed and into another,
never finding a man who can hold her;
her steady progress through the city's gentry
reduced to a sort of venereal mathematics
which finds its ultimate expression in a brothel.

If, however, you choose to be a mistress,
Vatsyayana advises you against
worrying about Gonardiya's homilies.
You should do as you please,
and follow wherever your heart leads you.

If you are high-born, ask your relatives
to render your lover favours
in proportion to the amount he has to spend
on your cocktail parties, cosmetics,
gifts to friends and bequests to temples.

There is no need for you to use or wear
the gifts your lover gives you.
Should you leave him of your own free will
you may keep only these things,
returning everything else that belongs to him.

When you move into your lover's house
you must quickly establish yourself as its ruler;
but stay on good terms with his wives,
and make a special effort
to fit in with the household's way of life.

Your role is very much the society hostess:
entertain his friends wittily,
and amuse them with displays of artistic skill;
at night, instruct his wives
in love techniques of which he is still ignorant.

As his mistress, it is your privilege
to reproach him for spending
too long in the company of whores,
for staying out all night,
or for doing anything else that annoys you.

In bed with him be utterly shameless,
using all your skills to arouse
and satisfy him, often taking the lead
without bothering to ask,
rolling him on his back to sit astride him.

Go out of your way to charm his wives,
honouring their children
with gifts of fine clothes and splendid jewels,
offering your services as nurse
or guardian whenever the opportunity arises.

You are his brilliant, if temporary, prize,
and must behave accordingly:
be magnanimous to his family and friends,
and allow yourself to be shown off
at parties, theatres, festivals and other events.

---

2. Vatsyayana uses the word *punarbhu*, which implies a virgin
widow who has remarried. But her position seems not to be like
that of other married women. She stands halfway between
them and courtesans, with less security but far more freedom
than a wife.

A Jaipur nobleman receives his mistress in a secluded lake pavilion. They have exchanged *paans* as a token of their love and she is offering him a glass of wine. The female attendants maintain a discreet aloofness. An excessive use of gold and ornamentation mark this as being a very late example of its school. *Jaipur, c.1850*

The Neglected Wife
If you are one of those unfortunate women
whose lives are made a misery
by the depredations of their co-wives,
you must seek the friendship
and assistance of your husband's favourite.

Care for her children as though you were
their nurse, and teach her
everything you know about the various arts –
helping her to please your husband
will help end his indifference to your plight.

Try also to win the affection of his friends,
and convey to him through them
that your love and loyalty are going unrewarded.
Lead the daily household prayers
and the *pujas*[3] on festivals and special feast-days.

With the other women, you should be retiring,
hiding your talents and never
allowing yourself to seem too good at anything;
always be very passionate in bed,
even if your husband leaves you utterly cold.

Never reproach or quarrel with your husband.
In fact, you should reconcile him
to wives with whom he has recently quarrelled,
and, if he desires another man's wife,
you should offer your services as go-between.

Quietly make yourself indispensable
to the success of his clandestine love-affairs;
keep his secrets, and act in such a way
that he cannot fail to recognize
and, ultimately, reward your loyalty.

Vatsyayana says that the wife who always
appears cheerful and who uses
Kama Sutra to intoxicate her husband with love
will always be his real favourite,
no matter how many wives compete against her.

---

3. See p. 116, note 3

A hill raja in his harem. He seems oblivious to the presence of
his wives and draws serenely on his *hookah*. One of the ladies
offers the inevitable *paan*. The *hookah* is far more often featured
in Pahari painting than in any other school. The stem was very
long and might coil through a bowl of orange or rose water, to
perfume the cool smoke. The difference of scale between the
raja and his wives reflects the difference in their rank, and is a
device common to all Indian schools. *Arki (Simla Hill State), mid
eighteenth century*

ROYAL WIVES

The conduct prescribed for eldest
and youngest wives,
and outlined in the previous chapter,
should be understood also
to apply to the ladies of the king's harem[1].

Each morning the chief eunuch of the harem
should appear before the king,
accompanied by maidservants bearing
garlands, perfumes and robes,
and announce which queens have sent these gifts.

Having accepted each present gracefully,
the king should send the maids
back to their ladies, each taking in return
some small token of his favour,
like flowers from the garlands he is wearing.

In the third watch of the afternoon the king
should go, richly dressed,
into the harem to pay surprise social calls
on those of his queens and ladies
whose company and conversation he most enjoys.

These visits, pleasant oases of laughter
amid the day's more onerous duties,
should be made, however, in the strictest order,
according to rank, and no visit
should last longer than each lady's status allows.

Having visited his legal wives in turn,
the king should tour the apartments
of his concubines and, finally, look in upon
the courtesans, singers, actresses
and dancers whom he has brought to the harem.

The suites of the royal queens should be
in the heart of the seraglio,
ringed by the apartments of the concubines;
the outermost rooms should be given
to the courtesans, actresses and dancing-girls.

The chief eunuch should prepare a daily list
of those queens and ladies
whose official turn it is to sleep with the king,
including those who have recently missed
their turns, and those who are in their *ritu* season[2].

He should then assemble the maidservants
of the ladies and lead the caucus,
which bears trays of perfumes and ornaments,
to the love-pavilion, where the king
will receive them when he wakes from his siesta.

One by one, each maidservant advances
to place before the king
her cargo of perfume-jars and jewels;
offerings which clearly display
the proud seal of her lady's signet ring.

When, at last, the king signifies
which gift he will accept,
the maids of the queen who sent it should race
to inform their lady that the king
will receive her that night in the love-pavilion.

When the ladies of the harem are assembled
to watch dancers, or hear a singer
during a religious festival, the king should order
wine served to all, and honour each,
according to her rank, with expensive presents.

---

1. The Sanskrit word is *antahapura* (inner city) which suggests
that ancient Indian kings kept their wives in a separate, fortified
building within the palace grounds. In Udaipur the *Zenana
Mahal* (Palace of the Queens) is built like a fortress and is
entirely windowless on the outside, the walls supported by
great towering buttresses almost a hundred feet high. At the
very top levels, lattice windows let in air and light. The queens'
apartments are decorated with gaily-coloured murals depicting
the love story of Radha and Krishna and with inlays and
mosaics. The palace is entered through two heavily-guarded
gateways and was considered so secure that it housed the state
treasury. The apartments of the chief queen stood above the
treasury and were called *Ranga Mahal* (the Painted Palace) and
Badala Mahal (Palace of the Clouds).

2. The monthly cleansing and, in particular, those days after
the period, from the fourth day on, which were considered to
offer the best chance of conception. 'Whoever does not make
love with his wife when she is in her *ritu* season must suffer the
pains of hell' (*Markandeya Purana* XIV 1). Both *Mahabharata* and
Ramayana count refusing a woman her *ritu* rights among the
most evil of all sins (*Ramayana* II 75: 52 and *Mahabharata* VII 17:
28–36).

A maharana of Udaipur leads his lover to a pavilion where the lovemaking couch awaits them. A servant carries the sword and shield from which he will never be parted. This garden, with its tall trees, is built on the highest part of Udaipur's *Zenana Mahal*, or Palace of Queens, some seven stories above ground level. From the pavilion the lovers will have a fine view across the Picchola Lake to the Jagnivas Palace (now the Lake Palace Hotel) and the Jagmandir Palace where Shah Jehan, builder of the Taj Mahal, took refuge from his father Jehangir. *Mewar, mid eighteenth century*

The ladies of the harem should never
be allowed to set foot outside,
nor should women of dubious character
be employed as palace servants;
only those of proven loyalty may be admitted.

When he is in bed with a lady the king
should be impeccable, an expert
and considerate lover; he needs to be an adept
of Babhravya's loving-arts
because he has so many ladies to satisfy.

Like any man who is husband to many women
he should treat them equitably,
neither neglecting nor favouring any one,
nor telling one about the blemishes
or peculiar sexual tastes of any other.

Likewise, he should not permit his wives
to quarrel, even when they appear
to have just cause; if any woman comes to him
with a complaint, he should hold her
to be the culprit, the pot calling the kettle black.

He must please his wives in different ways,
making a confidante of one,
delighting another with vows of love,
flattering a third in public,
taking a fourth riding with him in the forest.

A fifth may be called often to his bed,
a sixth honoured with gifts,
a seventh by favour shown to her relatives;
thus, shrewdly assessing each woman,
he should aim to win the affection of all.

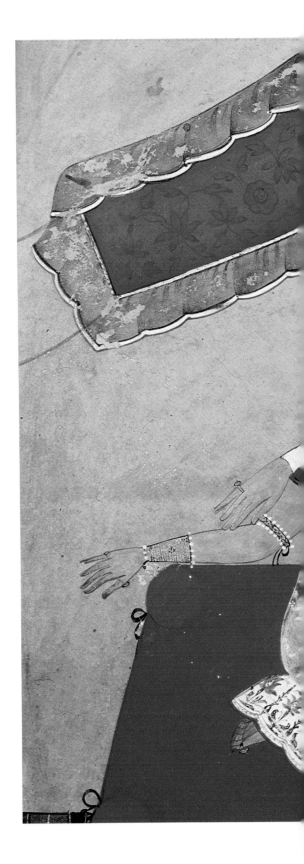

A prince of Mankot, in the Punjab hills, dallies with two of his
harem as a prelude, perhaps, to what Vatsyayana calls
Sanghataka (the Brace). The style of this miniature is pure
Basohli, which was the dominant school in the area until the
middle of the eighteenth century. *Mankot, c.1720 (detail)*

BOOK V
OTHER MEN'S WIVES

ILLICIT LOVE

The various excuses[1] suggested by Gonikaputra
for seducing another man's wife
have been discussed in an earlier chapter.
Lust is not one of them –
that is specifically and utterly condemned.

No matter how urgently you desire
a married woman, you may
not approach her unless it is beyond doubt
that your love must end
either in her bed or in your death.

The Ten Stages of Love[2]
You'll recognize a fatal love
by the way you keep hoping to catch her eye,
find yourself daydreaming about her
and then dreaming about her,
until the fever will not even let you sleep.

Next you'll be refusing food
brought to you by your loving wife;
you'll grow haggard;
old pleasures will seem worthless;
the company of former lovers will be an agony.

Soon your affairs will be in a mess;
you'll lose all dignity and
your friends will say 'he has gone mad!'.
Fainting fits will follow,
before death comes finally to close your eyes.

But even when you're convinced this fatal
passion is dragging you
remorselessly towards the grave,
there are still questions to be answered
before you enmesh yourself with her.

Is she honestly the right woman?
How well do they guard her?
Will she be easy to seduce?
Should you succeed, is there a future in it?
Will being found out ruin you?

Your first important decision,
if you're still determined to proceed,
is whether to involve
a messenger you can trust,
or make the initial approach yourself.

Whereas young girls, the sages say,
prefer to be approached by the man himself,
experienced adultresses,
who know the value of discretion,
should be approached through go-betweens.

But there's not a woman alive,
Vatsyayana believes,
who wouldn't much rather the thrilling conquest
of her emotions and her body
were begun by the ardent lover himself.

Only if she's locked away
in her *zenana*[3],
jealously guarded by her husband,
or is otherwise quite impossible to get at,
should you use a go-between.

Your first step, if you've chosen
to stalk her yourself,
is to get to know her socially.
This is easy if she and her husband are often
guests at your house, or vice versa.

Otherwise you must contrive to be
forever bumping into her – at a friend's house,
at the doctor's, her lawyer's,
at weddings, sacrifices, festivals and funerals,
at picnics and at garden parties.

When she is nearby, shoot her glances
full of brooding significance,
bite your lip and tug at your moustache,
file your nails to expert's points
and toy abstractedly with your rings and necklace.

Speak in her presence to your friends
of unrequited love, telling
anecdotes which ostensibly concern other ladies
but which are really aimed at her,
and convey your love of life and sexual pleasure.

Lie back in the lap of a woman friend,
yawning, stretching your limbs,
listening half-heartedly to what she is saying,
quizzing her languidly with your eyebrows,
murmuring the occasional deprecating remark.

---

1. See p. 34, including note 3. See Glossary for Gonikaputra.

2. This is a love so keen that it can kill, if unrequited. Love was thought to live in women's eyes, an idea which finds an echo, centuries later, in Chaucer's Troilus, who was 'ful unwar that Love hadde his dwellynge withine the subtile stremes of hir (Criseyde's) yen'. Perhaps, like chess, this idea found its way to

Europe with the returning crusaders. The notion that one can die of a broken heart is not as ridiculous as it sounds. It is not so many years since Prince Salar Jung of Hyderabad pined away and died for love of a lady who is now happily married and living in the West.

3. See p. 28, note 2

The lady in this delicate miniature is prostrated by pangs of unrequited love.
Fanning will not drive out her fever. Her pain will not be eased by massage. Her
maids carry flasks of useless medicine. The marble quern and grindstone can
prepare no healing drug. Even her jewelled *paan*-casket offers no solace. From her
demeanour one would judge her to have advanced at least four stages out of ten
towards death (see note 2, opposite); but there is always hope. *Garhwal, c.1780–1800*

Should a small child stray within reach
commandeer it and shower it
with the endearments you've been saving for her –
simple double-entendres like:
'I adore you darling, I wish you were mine.'

Leave her in no doubt of your meaning
by treating the child like a lover;
kissing its upturned face and caressing it,
giving it *paan*[4] from your tongue,
and chucking it tenderly under the chin.

With her child be even more effusive;
bring it toys to play with
(return these later to your own children),
and tell its mother constantly
that you see where her baby gets its beauty.

Cultivate her relatives and friends
and, should they prove sympathetic,
use them as a fifth column;
but see to it, in any case,
that you're a frequent visitor to her house.

Seated in her courtyard, launch
a debate upon the finer points of *Kama Sutra*,
ensuring that she can hear you
but that she does not suspect
you've begun the conversation for her benefit.

Ask her, as your friendship grows, to accept
some money for safekeeping;
retrieve it in tiny amounts and deposit
in its place, jewels and ornaments
that she will have to hold for a longer period.

Further your friendship with gifts
of betel-nuts, perfumes
and other little luxuries she needs daily,
sparing her the trouble of sending
her maid out to the *bazaar* when they are used up.

Arrange for her to visit your house
and sit gossiping and being
entertained in private by your wives.
The more often you meet her
the quicker romance will flower between you.

When she needs the services of goldsmiths,
gemcutters, jewel-polishers,
indigo and saffron dyers, carpenters and others,
introduce her to your own craftsmen
and have the work done under your supervision.

---

4. See p. 28, note 3

A crowned king dandles two children on his knee while two others play nearby, watched by four women holding sacred lotus flowers. The painting probably illustrates an episode from the *Bhagavata Purana*, the largest source of stories about the childhood of the blue-skinned god Krishna. Children are especially precious in India, where life is so uncertain, and are always made a great fuss of. This is why the legends of the mischievous child Krishna are so popular and also why it was so easy, neither forced nor obviously insincere, for Vatsyayana's reader to caress a passing child. *Rajasthani, eighteenth century*

When one project is almost completed,
launch another immediately.
In this way you can spend long periods
in her company without anyone
suspecting something is going on between you.

If she asks you how a job should be done,
or wishes she were skilled
in music, singing or any other of the arts,
teach her what she needs to know,
thus displaying your own talent and efficiency.

Sit with the lady and her servants,
amusing them with stories
from the epics and *puranas*[5],
discussing how to value precious stones
and recognize a first-quality silk.

Produce an uncut gem or scrap of fabric
and ask for a valuation,
appointing the lady arbiter in all disputes.
Let it be understood that you
consider her very wise, her judgement marvellous.

As friendship deepens into love you must begin
to woo her, subtly if she's innocent,
using the techniques prescribed for young virgins;
but if the lady is experienced
there's no point wasting her time with niceties.

When, from her expression as she speaks
and the language of her body,
you understand that she is falling in love,
give her some discreet love-token,
and ask for something you can treasure in return.

Implore her for a phial of her favourite perfume,
her ring or shawl, the garland
from around her neck or the betel quid
she has just placed in her mouth,
or beg the auspicious blue lotus from her hair.

You could give her an expensive perfume,
costly jewels she has admired,
or simply flowers and leaves imprinted
by your teeth and fingernails –
more eloquent of passion than any words.

Let these overtures, so slowly that she
scarcely even notices, become
increasingly intimate; and work very patiently
to anticipate and scotch any last
fears she may have about committing adultery.

When the time comes, take her secretly
to a safe place – a thickly wooded city garden,
barley fields in the distant countryside,
a jungle hillside, cave or riverbank,
or a ruined temple, bereft of its idols.

Offer her a *supari-paan*[6] from your lips
and kiss her passionately.
Embrace her and touch her breasts;
gently loosen the knot of her skirt;
caress her secret parts, and then enjoy her there.

While seducing someone else's wife
you should leave his other wives strictly alone;
only a lunatic would attempt two at once.
And any old women living in his house
will have to be bribed to keep their mouths shut.

If you know that a man is in the habit
of seeking sexual solace
in the arms of street walkers and prostitutes,
you should never approach his wife,
no matter how easily available she may be.

No man who values his reputation will,
if he has any sense, risk adultery
with a woman who is nervous, too well guarded,
afraid of her husband,
or who has a jealous, watchful mother-in-law.

---

5. Eighteen lengthy texts which are virtual encyclopaedias of myth and legend and which contain genealogies of gods, heroes and saints. The *Bhagavata Purana* is the main source of tales about Krishna.

6. A *paan* made with areca nut, which is mildly narcotic and is the produce of the areca palm.

A Bundi gentleman pays a social call on a lady and finds her seated with a friend
and servants on her terrace. The mood of the gathering, as evidenced by the
careless fluttering of the pigeons and the tameness of the *chakoras*, is very relaxed.
The man has been welcomed with a pair of lotus buds, and tastefully yet not too
lavishly entertained with pomegranates, grapes and flasks of wine or sherbets. An
attendant performs on a *dilruba. Bundi, c.1775*

TESTING HER FEELINGS

By carefully observing the lady's
gestures and behaviour when you meet,
you can deduce, fairly accurately,
whether or not she favours you.
If the signs are unfavourable, hire a go-between.

When, despite the fact that she
does not appear to encourage your advances,
she wishes to go on meeting you,
it means that she is caught in a dilemma
which only patience will resolve.

If she refuses to meet you secretly
and yet appears, the very next time you see her,
dressed more provocatively than before,
you may infer that she will yield,
but in private, and to a more forcible approach.

The woman who keeps several secret trysts
without succumbing to your desire
is probably trifling with your feelings
and will prove an arid conquest
when, eventually, she allows you to bed her.

Some ladies, having met you several times
(but having neither slept with you
nor refused directly to do so),
will suddenly break off the affair –
their honour is salved if they go no further.

But human beings are notoriously fickle,
and even when a relationship
appears to have broken down irretrievably,
it is usually not very difficult
to pick up and reassemble the fragments.

Those women who, despite their jealously
guarded self-respect, dream
secretly of lying in their lovers' arms
must have their resistance broken down
with the expert blandishments of a go-between.

A woman who meets you in secret,
only to manifest her lack of desire
and reject your advances with angry contempt,
should not be pursued further.
There are, however, exceptions even to this rule.

It is not unknown for a woman to rebuff
a man in the harshest terms
yet, later, relent and welcome him to her bed.
You should therefore be aware
of the myriad reasons that can cause rejection.

Reasons for Refusal

It is a man's nature, says Gonikaputra[1],
to desire every lovely woman he sees,
and a woman's to dream of every handsome man;
yet, for quite separate reasons,
promiscuity is very rare in either sex.

Most men, whether or not they admit it,
have at one time or another
secretly desired some other man's wife,
but have done nothing about it
because *Dharma* and Aryan law forbade them.

Women, on the other hand, rarely worry
about *Dharma* and *Adharma*[2];
they follow their hearts and lose them,
completely, when they have affairs.
There are other reasons for a woman's reticence.

It is in a woman's nature to retreat
when a man propositions her,
no matter how much she may desire him.
Also, she knows that unlike herself
he may grow indifferent once the chase is over.

Experience shows that men tend to despise
women who are easily available
and desire those who are difficult to seduce.
These reasons underlie most rebuffs,
but , of course, there are myriad others.

Even if the girl desires you,
loyalty to her husband
or to the milky-mouthed child at her breast
may decide her against you –
or she may fear you're simply trifling with her.

She may, if she's suffered a bereavement,
be too miserable to think of love.
Maybe she simply lacks opportunity because
her husband is always there,
Perhaps she's too old to be excited by infidelity.

She may realize that, whatever happens,
she will never wholly own you;
or suspect that your heart is really elsewhere
and that before long you'll drift
away from her and into some other woman's arms.

If you're a gossip, she may fear scandal.
Do you, perhaps, trust too deeply
in your friends, telling them your secrets,
and valuing only their advice?
Or could she suspect you're not entirely sincere?

---

1. See Glossary

2. *Adharma* is whatever contradicts *Dharma*, for a fuller
discussion of which see Introduction.

The storm has prevented her lover from keeping their tryst, so the lady stands at the door, her empty bed behind her. Indian aesthetes know her as *vasakasajja nayika*, the waiting heroine. Although she chiefly expresses loneliness and yearning, the painter could also make her angry, fearful, confident, just as he liked. The lady of this dramatic painting seems to symbolize the complexity of feeling with which Vatsyayana has to deal in this chapter. *Poonch, Punjab Hills, c.1780*

It's possible that she thinks you're too noble,
too powerful or prominent for her;
or, if she's the deer type[3], simply too big.
Perhaps you make her feel
her lack of sophistication and skill in the arts.

If you are an old friend, it's likely
that she doesn't want to spoil your friendship.
Or perhaps you lack finesse, possessing
absolutely no sense of occasion,
or you come from a low or a dubious family?

She may consider you a peasant
if you can't see when she's encouraging you.
Or, if she's passionate and a *hastini*[4],
she may have heard gossip
that you're undersexed and undersized.

If she loves you very deeply she may fear
for your safety or reputation.
Or perhaps she is honest enough to recognize
that the liaison couldn't work,
not because of your faults, but her own.

She may be terrified that, if the affair
becomes public gossip,
she will be disowned by her relatives.
Or you may simply have forgotten
to dye your grey hairs before you approached her.

Finally, she may suspect that her husband
has sent you to try her loyalty.
Of course, it is possible that none of these
is the case, but that she wishes
to turn away her face from such bad *Dharma*.

Encouraging Signs
If the lady permits you to caress her,
but feigns ignorance of your true intentions,
you will know that she is torn
between passion and reason;
you must therefore be patient and considerate.

If, when she is lying drowsily on a bed,
you place your hand on hers,
and she, pretending to be asleep, does not object,
but snatches it away when she wakes,
you may interpret this as a sign of encouragement.

After this you can gradually advance
to squeezing her feet with yours,
and lying beside her caressing her body.
She will put a stop to this when she wakes,
but it's a good sign if she isn't very angry.

A woman in the grip of strong desire
behaves with a sort of childish petulance;
she will find any excuse to uncover
her beautiful temptress's limbs,
and speaks to you in a low, tremulous stammer.

You will notice beads of sweat pearling
her lovely face and hands.
When she offers to massage your head
her hands will stray to your body
and her thighs will press hard against yours.

She will press your feet with one hand
while the other roams your body,
its caresses growing steadily more intimate;
her breathing grows harsh and unsteady
despite the fact that you've not touched her.

Complaining of exhaustion, she leaves
both her hands on your thighs
and rests her forehead heavily upon them.
Sooner or later her hands
will move, but it won't be towards your feet.

She will, with casual elegance, lay
one hand upon your groin
and leave it there, paying it no attention
until, provoked beyond restraint,
you squeeze it powerfully between your thighs.

She will return to massage you
as often as you ask her,
but will never make a more blatant approach.
It is for you to understand
that she will not now reject your caresses.

If a woman shows every sign of desire
and yet is impossible to bed,
you must decide whether her amorous behaviour
reflects her deeper feelings
or whether she is amusing herself at your expense.

If, on the other hand, she receives
your signals, innuendoes
and advances with complete indifference,
you must either give her up
or solicit the aid of a professional go-between.

Some women are too stupid to take hints
or too suspicious to respond,
yet this is not proof positive that they
utterly reject your love –
all you need is the patience of an ox.

3, 4. See p. 42, notes 1 and 2

The successful adulterer. The man is sitting in a basket which
his lover is hauling, singlehanded, up towards her turret
window. Behind her, the empty bed awaits. The tame peacocks
and monkeys of the park present no threat to the lovers, but of
the other pets mentioned in *Kama Sutra,* the parrot and the
mynah were notoriously indiscreet. This painting belongs to
the same set as the one reproduced on page 49. *Sirohi,
eighteenth century* (*detail*)

THE ARTS OF THE GO-BETWEEN

If the lady's behaviour proclaims
her willingness to meet you,
but you dare not arrange a tryst
or speak openly to her,
you must employ a seasoned go-between.

The go-between, who should be well-known
to the lady you wish to enmesh,
will spend a few days winning her confidence,
praising her beauty and character,
before she settles down to her real business.

Once secure in the lady's trust,
she will bring out illustrated manuscripts
of various romantic and erotic texts,
reading first from the sections
which give beauty-tips and recipes for cosmetics.

Next, she will read from the chapters
which chronicle the adulteries
of heroes like Brihaspati, high-priest to the gods,
who slept with his brother's wife,
and Lord Indra, who cuckolded the sage Gotama[1].

Thus, subtly, the go-between winds
towards the arts of lovemaking,
eulogizing the lady's talent in these arts
and saying how rarely such skill
is found combined with character and beauty.

She will say, in fake astonishment:
'How can such a beautiful,
talented and charming woman as yourself
have ended up with such a husband?
Lovely lady, he's not fit to be your servant!'

'No-one can understand', she continues,
'why you put up with a man
who is jealous, devious, weak, cold as a fish –
an ungrateful, manic-depressive,
indifferent lover who isn't even faithful.'

The go-between exaggerates his flaws
and, to get his wife confused and demoralized,
paints his character black as it is pure,
relying on half-truths to give credence
to the lies that gradually destroy his wife's love.

If, however, the lady is the deer type[2],
the go-between is not so foolish
as to point out that her husband is a hare –
since they're perfectly matched.
(To claim that he's a horse would be ridiculous).

But if, from interviews with his old lovers,
the go-between discovers that the man
is a hare while the lady is a mare or an elephant[3],
she will use this fact to belittle
whatever pleasure the lady gets from lovemaking.

When she judges that the woman's loyalty
to her husband is faltering,
the go-between takes her aside and says:
'Listen carefully, lovely one,
I'm going to tell you something astonishing.'

Now, for the first time, she mentions
your name and lineage, saying:
'Since he met you, lady, he's been utterly mad.
Poor fellow, he's so soft-hearted –
never in his life has he suffered such agonies.'

'He won't touch food, and no longer sleeps.
If he can't win your love, my dear,'
the go-between continues gravely,
studying the lady's face,
'the miserable fellow will very likely die!'

If, despite herself, the lady's eyes
sparkle and she seems pleased,
the go-between relates how folk-heroines
like Ahalya, Kurangi and Shakuntala[4]
responded, in similar situations, to their lovers.

She also praises your vigour, beauty, charm
and expertise in the arts of love,
telling the lady that no man is better suited,
physically and by temperament,
to please her in all three stages of lovemaking.

Next, as proof of your desirability,
she names a lady famous either
for her incomparable beauty or icy virtue
and claims, whether or not it's true,
that this lady seduced you and was your lover.

---

1. See Glossary

2, 3. See p. 42, notes 1 and 2

4. See Glossary

144

The use of go-betweens is a recurring theme in Indian art and literature. The love of Radha and Krishna, in particular, would have been impossible but for the indefatigable Sakhi who carried endless angry messages back and forth between them. The go-between in this powerful illustration to the *Amarushataka* has been sent by King Amaru to make his excuses to the dejected lady. Other paintings in this series are on pages 91 and 175. *Malwa, c.1680*

During these sessions, the go-between
watches very carefully
for signs that tell her she is succeeding –
the lady smiles, laughs aloud,
meets the other's eyes without embarrassment.

She calls the go-between to sit beside her
and asks, solicitously:
'Where have you been? Are you rested?
What have you been doing?
Have you eaten? Whom have you been seeing?'

When they're alone, she no longer bothers
to disguise her loneliness,
and begins to unfold the story of her life;
she yawns nervously and sighs,
often seeming distracted, lost in daydreams.

She sends for the go-between at festivals
and whenever she has an excuse
to employ her on various trifling errands,
rewarding her handsomely each time
and, when she leaves, asking her to come again.

The lady will angle for compliments
by salting their conversations
with sly, self-deprecating remarks like:
'You're a truthful woman,
so why tell me these incredible stories?'

She protests that your devotion
is all cunning humbug,
your character sieved through with faults,
and that nothing in the world
could induce her to set one foot in your direction.

If the go-between speaks of your Great Love,
she laughs and cries, 'Ridiculous!',
dismissing your hopes as utterly vain.
Signs like these, beyond any doubt,
signify the success of the go-between's mission.

Unlike Svetaketu Auddalaki[5], who says
go-betweens are useless to couples
who have not met before, Vatsyayana believes
their true role is as catalysts,
creating love between two perfect strangers.

Well before you have met your lady
the go-between can take her
paan, saffron, flower-garlands, rings,
fine clothes, lovely silks
and any other presents you wish to send.

Each flower in the garland will bear
marks of your nails and teeth, the costly silks
will be wrapped in a cloth upon which
she finds a clear message of love –
your palmprints made in yellow saffron dye.

She discovers, tucked inside a headdress
of intricately woven jasmine,
fresh leaves which when unfolded display
glyphs, made by your fingernails,
depicting a couple: angry, sorrowful, making love.

The go-between, ferrying these presents
back and forth between you,
watches love flowering in both hearts
and, eventually, arranges
the tryst that ends her own employment.

The followers of Babhravya[6] say
that secret trysts are best planned to coincide
with pilgrimages, visits to temples,
picnic expeditions to the forest
or the mass bathing on the eve of an eclipse.

They advise meeting in the throngs
at weddings, sacrifices, festivals and funerals,
among crowds watching a house burn down,
criminals being caught and executed
or the royal elephants swaying past in processions.

Gonikaputra[7] says that trysts may safely
be arranged at the houses of friends,
beggarwomen, prostitutes and nuns;
but Vatsyayana thinks that, given
a secret exit, her house is the safest place of all.

5, 6, 7. See Glossary

A pair of lovers meeting secretly at a forest pavilion are
disturbed by thirsty lions. The lovers, who look as unconcerned
as the lions, calmly prepare to defend themselves, the proud
Rajput nobleman seizing the chance to demonstrate two skills
at once. *Rajasthani, eighteenth century*

THE WIVES OF SUBORDINATES

Kings, princes, noblemen and ministers
of the royal court must never
force their way into the houses of common folk –
the behaviour of the great
sets standards for the rest of the nation.

Just as the creatures of the living three worlds
wake each morning as the sun lifts
over the horizon and curl up to sleep
only after the sun has set,
so commoners follow the example of kings.

For this reason alone it is vital
that kings, princes and other powerful men
should never stain their honour
with such foul practices
as the seduction of other people's wives.

But should any man in authority be caught
in the grip of overwhelming need,
or if his life is threatened by his passion,
there are certain ways and means
which can be used to minimize the damage.

The wives and daughters-in-law of villagers
may be had by the village headman,
the local commissioner of taxes and the officer
in charge of agricultural records
without difficulty, simply by saying the word.

The *vitas*[1] call these women *charshanis*[2] –
the ceaselessly labouring wombs
of the Aryan race, selfless beings whose lives
are dedicated to nurturing seed,
whether it is sown in fields or in their bellies.

These amiable women are accosted and enjoyed
when they're grinding corn or spices,
pounding grain, entering houses and barns
to store and remove foodstuffs,
and while on their way to work in the rice-paddies.

Also when they appear at the gate
offering to card and spin raw wool and cotton,
crush linseed for oil, weave jute and hemp
into ropes and sacks; while buying
and selling these things, or when summoned.

Similarly, officers in charge of dairies
coerce the women who churn curds,
and officials who administer the *khadi*[3] industry
force the widows, nuns and destitutes
who take in spinning to earn their meagre livings.

The soldiers of the nightwatch blackmail
women out on the streets at night
by threatening to expose their guilty secrets;
the officers in charge of markets
compel women who come to sell flower-garlands.

In the cities of Pattana, Nagara and Kharvata[4],
citizens' wives are asked to the palace
each eighth day of the waxing moon,
on Kama's day and at Sharad Purnima[5]
to be entertained by the ladies of the harem.

They are welcomed with drinks and snacks
and, after introductions are made,
go off in pairs with the harem ladies
to sit gossiping in corners
until evening, when they return to their homes.

Should the king desire a married woman,
he sends a palace maid to request her presence
at one of these festivals and to promise
that when she visits the palace
she will be taken on a tour of its attractions.

When, in the evening, the woman prepares
to return to her home, she is met
by the same maid, who offers to conduct her
around the palace and gardens
and point out everything of beauty and interest.

The woman will be shown mosaics of coral,
emerald-inlaid floors, crystal walls,
the gardens of flowering and fruiting trees,
and delicate marble pavilions
whose pillars are wreathed with grape vines.

The lake pavilion with water flowing
in its conduits and fountains,
secret passages inside the castle walls,
halls of murals and the park
with its sprinklers and herd of tame deer.

The collection of mechanical warriors
and animals, so perfectly made
that they seem alive, the tame swans, partridges,
and the royal menagerie with its
caged tigers, lions and other wild animals.

When the woman is thoroughly impressed,
the maid tells her in confidence
that the king desires her very ardently,
adding that, as she may have heard,
he is a great expert in the art of lovemaking.

---

1. See p. 32, including note 14

2. I have tried to tease out the pun that must have been intended in this word. The *charshanis* are the daughters of Aryaman, progenitor of the Aryans. The word also means 'cultivator' and 'disloyal wife'.

3. Small scale spinning and handloom industry. *Khadi* cloth is what every Indian politician wears in an effort to be one of the 'people'.

4. See Glossary

5. The full moon of October. The most important night of the year in Agra, when a full scale fair is held in the grounds of the Taj Mahal

A Mughal prince, out on a hunting expedition, receives water at a country well. Shy village girls hasten to help him, pouring carefully from a spouted clay pot. Their own pitchers lie temporarily forgotten in the excitement. It was women like these that the *vitas* of Vatsyayana's day referred to as *charshanis*, easy conquests. This theme, which is very popular in Mughal painting, may have originated with a story of two lovers called Shahid and Wafa, who were supposed to have met in this way.

Mughal, c.1720

Once the king has enjoyed the woman
the maid calls again for her and conducts her
out of the palace, assuring her that,
apart from the three of them,
no-one else will ever know what happened.

If the woman should refuse, the king
comes himself to welcome her
and, after he has had his way, dismisses her
affectionately, sending her home
laden with expensive presents for her family.

Should her husband be eminent enough
to deserve favour at court,
the king will honour all his wives
with the royal invitation,
thus creating an alibi for the one he desires.

Or else the favourite queen, on the pretence
of seeking her friendship,
will summon the woman to the harem
and drug her with honeyed wine
so that the king can enter and enjoy her there.

If the woman is known for her fine voice,
or skill at playing the *vina*[6],
the harem ladies will call her to perform for them
and then send a maid to show her
round the palace and into the king's bedroom.

Should her husband fear the king's anger,
or have suffered some loss,
a maid from the harem visits her and says:
'Let me take you to meet my lady
and we'll soon have your husband out of trouble.'

'This queen', she continues, 'loves me dearly
and always listens to my advice –
she is so sweet and merciful by nature
that she's bound to help you',
and the maid leads the woman into the harem.

After two or three pleasant meetings,
the queen pledges her help
and the king restores the husband's fortunes.
While the woman is still elated,
they corrupt her, using one of the earlier methods.

It is simple for a king, by these means,
to seduce the wives of those
who are seeking employment in the royal service,
who are plagued by his tax-collectors,
or who have been unjustly or forcibly arrested.

Equally vulnerable are the wives of men
who have lost actions in the courts,
who are ambitious for status, power or honours,
who are oppressed by rich landowners,
or who, like spies, dare not risk the king's enmity[7].

If a king takes a fancy to a woman
who, although married,
is living openly with her lover,
he can simply order her
arrested, enslaved and placed in his harem.

If, on the other hand, the woman is in love
only with her lawful husband,
the king can fabricate evidence against the man,
execute him as an enemy-of-state,
and place his grieving widow in the harem.

These secret practices are commonest
among wild, young princes.
But no king who cares about his good name
should ever enter the house
of another man intending to seduce his wife.

Abhira[8], King of Kotta, was assassinated
by a washerman while he was busy
cuckolding Vasumitra under Vasumitra's roof.
Jayasena, King of Kashi, was killed
in flagrante delicto by his cavalry commander.

But in certain countries which still
hold to their ancient customs,
kings are permitted to enjoy other men's wives –
and this is done quite openly,
with the full consent of their husbands.

An Andhra bride bears gifts to the palace
on the tenth day of her marriage
and spends the tenth night in the king's bed.
At Vatsagulmaka, in the south, the king
sleeps with wives of his generals and ministers.

The foregoing are the chief techniques
used by the rulers and noblemen
of various lands for seducing other men's wives;
but a king who values his people's welfare
should never stoop to these disgraceful practices.

He should outlaw and abolish any hoary old
customs which, having come tumbling
down the ages, still plague his kingdom today.
Only if he defeats the six enemies
of mankind[9] can he have a happy, fruitful reign.

---

6. See p. 28, note 4

7. The art of spying was highly developed in ancient India and has two chapters devoted to it in Kautilya's *Arthashastra*. The king employed spies both to collect information in foreign countries and to report on the behaviour of his own subjects.

8. See Glossary for Abhira and all the proper names that follow.

9. The six enemies of mankind are Lust, Anger, Greed, Hypocrisy, Pride and Jealousy.

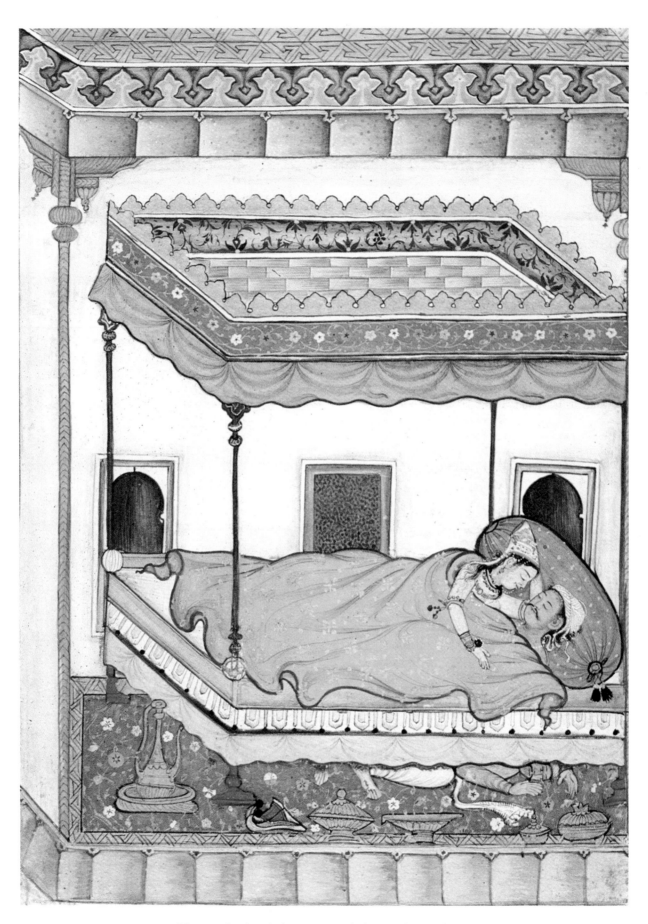

The sort of undignified situation in which even a king might
find himself if he wished to avoid the fate of Abhira and
Jayasena. The miniature illustrates a story in the
Anwar-i-Suhayli and the Persian text is equally caustic about
those above and below the mattress. *Mughal, 1570*

BREAKING INTO THE HAREM

Since harems are well-guarded and no man
is ever permitted to enter one,
the queens, who outnumber the solitary king,
cannot all be physically satisfied,
and must depend on each other for their pleasure.

They may dress their slave-girls as men,
adorn them with male jewelry,
and lie beneath them taking their pleasure
with artificial aids fashioned from
tubers, roots, fruits and other such things.

The king also, out of pity for his ladies,
will often strap on a phallus
and pleasure several of them in one night.
He is himself only with favourites
and those, newly-bathed, who are in their *ritu*[1].

Men too, when deprived of women,
have been known to satisfy
their desire with mares, ewes and bitches,
artificial *yonis*[2], statues,
lifesize dolls, masturbation and pederasty.

The ladies of the seraglio are adept
at smuggling in beardless youths dressed as girls –
their maids go in search of gentlemen
who can be bribed to dress
in women's clothes and sneak into the harem.

Should one of these women approach you,
she will claim that it is easy
to enter the harem, that the guards are careless,
that the palace has hundreds of hidey-holes,
and that the king very seldom visits his ladies.

If there were no safe escape route, the women
would be suicidally foolish to let you in;
but, says Vatsyayana, never enter a king's harem,
no matter how safe it seems –
the danger is great, and it threatens your life.

If you must enter, make sure you understand
the escape route perfectly, that
the harem gives on to a thickly-forested garden
with long and widely-separated avenues,
and that its guards are few and very careless.

Go only when the king is out of town
and after a queen has sent for you
a number of times, promising a rich reward;
even then, don't go unless she sends
a servant to guide you to and from her suite.

Of course, if all these conditions obtain daily,
you may come and go as you please,
but as a regular visitor to the harem
you will have to befriend the guards
if you're to prevent them becoming suspicious.

A credible excuse might be that you're
trying to seduce a palace maid
(point out the personal maid of your lover);
appear miserable when she cannot meet you –
this will amuse the guards enormously.

This girl and other palace maids should
be enlisted as your messengers;
you must also, for your safety's sake,
be able instantly to recognize
every informer and spy in the royal service.

If your messages cannot be passed on,
stand near the palace gates,
or where your lady can see you from her window;
but be sure to catch her eye,
otherwise there's little point in standing there.

If the guards begin to get restless,
remind them of your fickle girlfriend, the maid;
and only when you see your lady's gaze
constantly touching you
should you discreetly make some sign to her.

On a wall in clear view of her window
paint a giant man and woman, and underneath
leave a punning poem scratched on a leaf
for her maid to find, also balls,
dolls, toys, a ring, all marked with nails and teeth.

Wait for messages in some busy city street
where her maid often shops,
and only when she comes to tell you
that it will be safe that night
should you visit your lady in the harem.

You can enter the palace at night
disguised as a guardsman,
or your lover can send her maid
to shepherd you in and out, wrapped
in the coarsespun *sari* of a village woman.

You can pass into the palace undetected
using the *tantric yoga* of *Putaputa*[3],
which will make you and your shadow invisible:
find a mongoose's heart, fenugreek,
a white-flowered gourd and the eyes of a snake.

---

1. See p. 128, note 2

2. The female sexual organs.

3. *Putaputa* means 'wrapped up, enclosed, enveloped'. See Glossary for *tantras*.

A heavy air of boredom and frustration hangs over this harem scene, painted in
Jodhpur by Amardas, the son of Naraindas. An inscription on the reverse claims
that one of these languid ladies is Aurangzeb's queen Zebunnissa, but this seems
unlikely. Some young queens, married to ageing rulers, did not even have time to
grow bored with the sybaritic existence. When Maharaja Man Singh died in 1843,
no less than six queens mounted the funeral pyre with his corpse. *Jodhpur, late
eighteenth century*

Smoke these ingredients, then grind them
in equal quantities to lampblack –
applying it to your eyes will make you vanish.
If these things are hard to find,
use a potion of lotus, country fig and sacred water.

At *Diwali*[4] you should take a lighted lamp
and join the bustling crowds
coming and going on the road to the palace –
slip in through a side-door and,
later, sneak out again to rejoin the revellers.

Other good times to enter the palace are:
when the gates are opened for bulk deliveries
or so that a wagon can be loaded;
during fetes and festivals,
when streams of people are constantly arriving.

When the maids are scurrying in confusion
upon some important errand;
when, because somebody is changing apartments,
goods are moved from one gate to another;
during the changing of the guard.

When scores of courtiers ride off to a picnic;
when the king sets out on a pilgrimage
or leaves with his troops on a long campaign:
at times like these bold young men
can easily enter and leave the palace unobserved.

The harem ladies know each other's secrets
and are united by a bond of guilt;
the cabal corrupts women hitherto faithful
and draws them into its circle,
deriving its security from the common danger.

In Aparantaka[5] no man is permitted in the harem
and so the women smuggle in
handsome, lustful, foolhardy young men –
an easy task, since their harems
are inadequately and carelessly guarded.

When King Abhira was ruling Kotta, the harem
used to entrap the *kshatriya*[6] guards.
The southern ladies of Vatsagulmaka's palace
dress their young beaux as girls
and whisk them past the guards into the harem.

In the Vidarbha palace, the queens entertain
all the young royal princes,
with the sole exceptions of their own sons.
In Strirajya, the royal women
sleep only with their kinsmen and clansfolk.

The queens of Gauda sleep with *brahmins*[7],
friends, ministers and slaves.
In Sind, the queens satisfy their desire
with doorkeepers, fanbearers
and any other males with business in the palace.

In the Himalayan kingdoms of the northwest,
young men bribe the guards
and go with friends to visit the harem ladies.
In Prachya eight or ten ladies will kidnap
a young man and hide him inside for weeks.

In Anga, Banga and Kalinga, the holy *brahmins*
go with rice, flowers and saffron
to bless the harem ladies, but always end up,
so it's said, copulating with them,
despite the curtains meant to keep them apart.

These are the arts of entering a harem,
and they complete the book
on seducing the wives of other men:
this part of *Kama Sutra* shows
how carefully men should look after their wives.

Babhravya says you should test your wife
by hiring a man to tempt her,
but Vatsyayana's reply is that as wicked people
have often led innocent girls astray,
only an idiot would risk corrupting his own wife.

A wise man will study the techniques
for seducing married women
which have been set down in this *Kama Sutra*:
if he understands them fully,
he will never be deceived by his own wife.

This work clearly shows how adultery
corrupts both men and women,
ruins their characters, destroys *Dharma* and *Artha*[8].
Men and women with any wisdom
will never even think of doing these evil things.

This part of *Kama Sutra* has been written
with the aim of helping husbands
and safeguarding the virtue of their wives:
it is not to be used for deception,
or to steal away the love of any man's wife.

---

4. Vatsyayana uses *ratri-kaumudi* (Kaumudi night) which, from the context, appears to be the autumn fire festival that we have identified with *yaksha-ratri* (Night of the Yakshas), for which see p. 30, including note 8, and p. 116, note 9. *Kaumudi* can refer to any moonlight festival.

5. See Glossary for Aparantaka and the other names that follow.

6. Men of the warrior caste

7. Priests

8. In their narrowest meanings, virtue and wealth respectively. See p. 18, note 1 and Introduction

A lady waits anxiously on a moonlit palace terrace with her attendants as her lover hauls himself up a rope of knotted linen they have let down for him. At the foot of the wall his horse waits, held by a servant. The eerie moonlight tones, deep shadows and angular lines all contribute to the sense of danger. *Lucknow Mughal, late eighteenth century*

BOOK VI
COURTESANS

CHOOSING A LOVER

Sleeping with strangers for gain does not
come naturally to women,
yet to succeed as a prostitute you must
disguise your love of money
as a natural desire for the man himself.

Never mind how cold he leaves you:
make love to each client as though he were
Kama[1] incarnated in your bed.
Sexual flattery
is the shortest route to a man's heart.

Prove to him that he, not his money,
inspires your divine lust
by always seeming selflessly devoted.
Don't be too obviously grasping;
use your wits and fleece him intelligently.

Some Practical Advice
You should at all times be well-dressed
and carefully made-up;
eyes upon the road outside your house,
ready to telegraph an invitation
to any passing gentleman who takes your fancy.

Place yourself where those who come and go
can catch a glimpse of you,
but don't display yourself too blatantly –
all too often prostitutes behave
like objects for sale in the *bazaar*.

Employ a pimp capable of attracting
sophisticated lovers,
inveigling them away from other girls,
helping you through hard times
and protecting you if a customer turns nasty.

Make allies of the city-guards,
lawyers and astrologers;
stay friendly with the local bully-boys,
your dance and music students,
the other girls and with your madam.

In addition you should cultivate
pithamardas, *vitas* and *vidushakas*[2],
garland-makers, perfumiers and wine-merchants,
hairdressers, washermen, beggars
and any others who could be useful to know.

Choosing a Lover
The ideal lover is, of course, young,
free of family ties
and fantastically rich,
able to spend his money as he likes –
preferably on you.

Young men who have recently
inherited large fortunes from their fathers
make perfect lovers;
not having earned the money themselves
they have no trouble spending it.

You will find rich pickings
in middle-aged men whose one obsession
is to hang on to their youth
and in men who are impotent
but who'd rather die than let the fact be known.

Look out for wealthy playboys,
astrologers, doctors, foreign mercenaries,
men who have the ear of the king
and guilt-ridden ascetics
who will always want to visit you on the sly.

If your dream is to be a hetaira
like Ambapali, with whom the Buddha[3] dined –
famous for your virtue, cherished
by princes and philosophers –
choose your present lovers with great care.

Take only the eminent and artistic:
men of noble birth,
university professors, learned *brahmins*
and courtiers astute enough
to know which way the wind's blowing.

Let your house be a home from home
for young poets and musicians,
famous writers, ballad singers, painters,
master craftsmen, story tellers
and bon viveurs noted for their wit.

Of these choose a man who is courteous,
generous, kind to friends,
who neither gossips nor neglects the gods;
take this man as your lover
and let your ambition ride upon his.

---

1. See Glossary

2. See p. 32, including note 14

3. See Glossary

Every courtesan needs to make her fortune fast: 'Dark and long-lidded, my eyes
were bright and flashing as jewels; now in old age they are dulled and dim. Once
my hands were smooth and soft, and bright with jewels and gold; now in old age
they twist like roots. Once my body was lovely as polished gold; now in old age it is
covered all over with tiny wrinkles.' From a Pali poem by Ambapali of Vaishali,
translated by Professor A. L. Basham. *Rajasthani, late eighteenth century*

So much the better if your lover shines
at social gatherings,
loves speaking in public debates
and going to parties
(never forgetting to take you with him).

He should be healthy, slim and strong,
gallant, never jealous,
not enslaved by liquor, drugs or other women,
ardent and yet gentle in bed
but, above all, an independent spirit.

Avoid men who suffer from leprosy,
tuberculosis, parasites
and other infectious diseases;
do not take a lover
whose breath or whose language is foul.

Shun misers, cruel or violent men,
thieves, sorcerers, spies,
any man disowned by his parents,
men who care nothing for their honour,
and men who are in love with their wives.

Qualities of Great Courtesans

The greatest courtesans are beauties
with alluring youthful bodies,
sweet voices and charming manners.
They adore lovemaking,
and value a man's character above his wealth.

Neither tricking nor deceiving their lovers,
faithful and self-possessed,
these girls are connoisseurs of the arts,
devoted to the gods
and welcome at every society gathering.

Although you may never know their success,
you should emulate them,
behaving modestly and intelligently,
avoiding quarrels and arguments,
knowing when to act and when to leave alone.

A great courtesan does not beg or importune,
never dresses or acts indecently
or does anything that might be considered vulgar;
she is careful to discourage gossip,
and has a hatred of dullness and stupidity.

She does not obtrude herself in conversation,
is never discourteous,
and is always grateful for what she receives.
Above all she is an expert
in *Kama Sutra* and its subsidiary arts and sciences.

Why Girls Become Prostitutes[4]

What possible reason, the sages ask,
could induce a girl to lose
her chastity and become a prostitute?
Her natural promiscuity?
Coercion? A desire to be wildly wealthy?

The urge to spite a rival, or be revenged
on her lover, or on her family?
Could sheer curiosity have led her in?
Or a great sorrow driven her?
Did she conceive it to be her religious duty[5]?

Was she acting out of compassion
for some lonely man?
Or acceding to a close friend's entreaty?
Did she yield to a man
who resembled somebody she had once loved?

Has she allowed herself to be spoiled
because she loves notoriety?
Or because she's too shameless to care?
Or even, if she used to be respectable,
because a determined man corrupted her?

Was she persuaded by promises
of wealth and honour?
Or because he was all she had in the world?
Did a lover refuse to marry her?
Or was she seduced by a relative or neighbour?

---

4. Every reason in this list occurs also in a recent (1962) study of prostitution in Bombay. Other causes unearthed by this study are neglect and ill-treatment by girls' parents or relatives, unhappy marriages, desertion by husbands and the actual connivance of parents and relatives. For Vatsyayana's coercion we may possibly also read the modern crime of kidnapping girls from remote villages and holding them prisoner in city brothels.

5. Vatsyayana simply mentions *Dharma* at this point, but he must be referring to the custom of dedicating young girls as temple prostitutes (*devadasis*). That the custom was prevalent centuries before Vatsyayana's time is shown by a Mauryan

inscription in a cave at Ramgarh which reads: 'the excellent young man Devadinna, the painter, loved Sutanuka, the slave-girl of the god.' In Damodara Gupta's *Kuttani Mata* the exquisite young prince Samarabhata, whom we have met taking *paan* on p. 102, note 5, was told by the dancing master of the *devadasis* of a Benares temple not to expect much of their dancing as their time was almost entirely occupied with amorous activities. According to the study mentioned in note 4, nearly one-third of Bombay's common prostitutes were *devadasis* (although they now have to dance in brothels, not temples) and over half of these were devotees of the mother goddess Yellama from what is now northern Katnataka.

Three elegant Hyderabad courtesans drinking wine on a
terrace. These ladies were not only beautiful, but expert singers
and dancers, with an almost encyclopaedic knowledge of Urdu
and Persian poetry. They were courted by princes and poets
alike, and could become vastly wealthy. *Hyderabad,
eighteenth century*

Vatsyayana says that these hypotheses
by themselves explain nothing.
To be a courtesan a girl must either be greedy
or desperate to escape poverty,
and she certainly needs a natural love of sex.

Before a girl compromises her chastity,
she should weigh the fear,
grief, rage, or whichever other emotion
seems so compelling to her,
against the inevitable outcome of her consent.

If she cannot decide whether her motive
is greed or desire, she will
delude herself less by assuming the former –
it is, after all, no sin
for a prostitute to combine business with pleasure.

Entrapping a Lover
Should any gentleman indicate
his wish to be your lover,
you must take your time before accepting him –
experience continues to prove
that men despise cheap goods.

The very first thing you must do
is to send your masseuse,
one of the singers from your retinue,
or a trusted *vidushaka*
to try and gauge his true intention towards you.

If these servants are not available
send a *pithamarda* to investigate
the man's personal habits, his feelings for you,
whether he keeps other girls
and, most important, the state of his finances.

Should you receive favourable reports
and your wishes match his,
despatch a *vita* to him with an invitation
to your house; the pretext
can be anything the *vita* chooses to improvise.

It will be quite enough to promise
a ram, cock or quail fight,
or that you have a wonderfully clever parrot,
or plan some entertainment
with singers, dancers, actors or musicians.

When he arrives at your house,
welcome him with a gift of such opulence
that he is overwhelmed with pleasure,
and be sure to let him know
that you took the trouble to choose it yourself.

Amuse him with witty conversation
on his favourite subjects,
and see that he is lavishly entertained.
When he leaves, have an especially
charming maid take another present to his house.

Send this girl often, armed with gifts
and honey-tongued speeches,
until at last the man returns to your house.
Thereafter, accompanied by a *pithamarda*,
you may visit his house as often as you choose.

When a lover enters your house,
the perfection of your *paans*,
flower-garlands and precious ointments
must fade before your beauty
and the elegance of your conversation.

The cold blaze in a diamond's heart
will awaken his affection,
but infinitely more precious are your glances,
heavy with unspoken desire,
that kindle the slow fires of his love.

Strange gifts capture his imagination,
his smile is easily won
by the artless chatter of your *pithamardas*,
but you must fetter his soul
before you bind your body to his in lovemaking.

A Lucknow dancing-girl of the mid nineteenth century, perhaps one of the ladies who presided over the debauchery at the court of Wajid Ali Shah, the last independent ruler of Oudh. The Lucknow courtesan (this one carries a highly ornate *vina*) and her tradition of witty, sophisticated entertainment, survived at least until Indian independence in 1947. The miniature, like its subject, is a trifle vulgar. The lamps on the wall are Victorian. *Lucknow, c.1840–50*

LIVING AS A WIFE

Once you've taken the man as your lover
you must be faithful,
behaving as if you were his only wife:
you should appear to love him
even if, in reality, you feel nothing.

Your mother must seem an avaricious dragon
who utterly despises the man;
any civility is a grave error of judgement.
(You should hire an old woman
to play this role if your real mother is dead.)

When you are sitting with your lover,
let 'mother' appear
and drag you forcibly from the room.
Feign hatred, fear, shame –
but never disobey her orders.

Or, to excuse yourself from his presence,
you can pretend to be ill.
But choose a disease which is credible,
not too disgusting, and which
may reasonably be expected to disappear quickly.

To soften his disappointment, let your maid
take him *paan*, cardamoms and flowers,
with a message saying that you are desolated
and would he please return the flowers
for you to kiss and caress in his absence.

When, tenderly embracing you in private,
he places a *paan* in your mouth,
exclaim delightedly that never in your life
have you tasted anything
quite so delicious or so beautifully folded.

When in bed with him pretend ignorance
of Babhravya's sixty-four arts –
'My love, I'm so inexperienced,
please teach me what to do' –
and use only the few techniques he can teach.

Prove yourself a willing pupil and sigh:
'Darling, you're so wonderful –
if only we could make love all night long!'
(If your genitals are blemished
or diseased, take care not to let him see.)

Afterwards, curled up together in bed,
lie nuzzling his shoulder.
Do not discourage his more intimate caresses
and, when he finally sleeps,
take him in your arms and kiss him lovingly.

Follow him with eyes full of longing
when he leaves in the morning.
Lean from your balcony till he's out of sight,
and duck back shyly if he sees you –
your confusion proves that your love is genuine.

You must learn to loathe his enemies
and champion his friends,
to share his triumphs and his sorrows,
and to show your desire by letting him
make love to you in the most unlikely places.

Throw the occasional jealous tantrum
about his wives and other women.
Claim, weeping, that the nail and tooth marks
you left on his body yesterday
were in fact made by some other woman.

Let your love for him remain unspoken,
expressed only in gestures.
Pretend, when he arrives, to be exhausted
or mad with grief, and whisper:
'What did you expect? You didn't come yesterday'.

Praise his more worthwhile activities
(building temples, digging wells) –
listen carefully when he talks of these things
and show your grasp of the subject
by asking informed, intelligent questions.

Compliment him on his witty conversation
and flatter his intellect
by deferring to him on almost every subject.
You should disagree strongly, however,
with his views on the question of polygamy.

Give him sympathy when he sighs deeply,
or loses at dice, or simply trips and falls.
Be quick with 'Bless you!' if he sneezes,
starts choking with laughter,
or jumps because a sudden noise has startled him.

Console him whenever he's depressed
and, whatever the cause,
say you also have been feeling low for weeks.
Never praise others in his presence
or criticize any man who shares his faults.

Let him constantly be noticing that you
treasure the gifts he made you.
If ever he unjustly accuses you of infidelity,
starve yourself and refuse
to wear any jewelry until he relents.

An argument over a lover. The girl in this beautiful Basohli miniature stands dejectedly outside her house, the very attitude of her body eloquent of her frustration. Her companion, in whom by a small stretch of the imagination we may see Vatsyayana's 'mother' character, is forbidding her to visit her lover. Striped trousers, in Basohli painting, are particularly associated with the court of Raja Kirpal Pal. *Basohli, c.1690–1700*

Cast off your jewels and refuse food
when some tragedy befalls him.
'Alas! how could this happen?', you should moan,
wringing your hands and suggesting
wild, impractical schemes to console him.

'Let's go, I beg of you, to a new country
where we can start all over again –
I could come with you if you offered to buy
my freedom from the king –
or else let's just run off together, tonight!'

Tell him again and again that meeting him
has given purpose to your life.
When, suddenly, he acquires wealth or property,
or recovers from a serious illness,
offer thanks to the gods with *pujas*[1] and fasts.

Always dress exquisitely to receive him,
and wear your finest jewels.
When asked to sing in public, weave his name
and the noble lineage of his clan
into the dedications which precede each song.

Your lover will be greatly moved
if, when you're not well,
you clasp his hand to your hot forehead,
or hold it to your heart
and fall asleep, as if soothed by his touch.

Sit often in his lap and doze off
with your head on his shoulder;
walk one pace behind him in the street;
say you want to bear his son:
all these stratagems are guaranteed to please.

Say that you pray daily to the gods
for death to take you first[2].
Beg him to stop whenever he fasts, saying,
'Let the sin be mine!';
but share his fast when he is adamant.

If you have another source of income
of which your lover is ignorant,
you must keep it a closely-guarded secret.
Always appear to husband
his resources as carefully as your own.

Should you be present at an argument
which neither side can resolve,
offer to send for your lover, saying:
'He will settle this fairly.
He is the only man I know who could.'

Let him see how humbly you adore him
by wearing his cast-off shawls
and gladly accepting leftovers from his plate.
Affect to be helpless without him,
never even going to parties on your own.

Exasperate your friends with eulogies
about his family, caste, country,
teacher, friends, age, virtue, wealth,
colouring, education, skills,
eloquence and anything else that leaps to mind.

No matter how laughable his talent
for singing, or performing
on the *vina, tabla*[3], flute or other instrument,
encourage him to play for you
and praise his uncommonly fine technique.

Once you have arranged a rendezvous
let nothing keep you from it,
even if the roads are too hot to walk,
the cold is too intense to bear,
or the eerie monsoon light threatens a cloudburst.

His every virtue, feeling and belief
should find its echo in you.
Accuse him of using witchcraft to enslave you
and say you hope to meet him again,
after death, and be his wife in the next life.

Quarrelling with 'mother' about your lover
should be part of your daily routine.
When she tries to coerce you into sleeping
with someone else, swear you will
take poison, fall on a knife, or hang yourself.

When your lover eventually discovers
that you have been unfaithful,
you must instantly despatch your maids
pithamardas, vitas and *vidushakas*[4],
to convince him that it's all your mother's fault.

---

1. See p. 116, note 3

2. Dying before one's husband is considered such a blessing by Indian women that the phrase *sadasuhagana*, which describes it, was recently used to advertise a brand of toilet soap!

---

3. A long-necked Indian lute, and small drum, respectively.

4. See p. 32, including note 14

The girl defies darkness, storms, snakes and the demons of the forest in order to keep a secret tryst with her lover. She stumbles through the night, oblivious to the fact that her golden anklets have been ripped off by thorns. To aesthetes, she is known as *abhisarika nayika*, the fearless lover. *Guler, c.1760*

If he will not be persuaded, go yourself,
and assure him of your devotion.
Weep, as you explain how 'mother' forced you.
Curse all prostitutes and lament
the fate that decreed this cruel life for you.

But however hysterically you may slander her,
never argue with 'mother' about money.
Be thankful that she will invariably send you
where the pickings are richest –
do absolutely nothing without her advice.

When Your Lover is Abroad
Say, crying, as your lover prepares to travel,
'Come back soon, or I'll die!'
Use no soaps, oils or cosmetics while he's away,
and wear no ornaments besides
your *mangala*[5] beads and one conch-shell bangle.

Remember his parting words fondly,
and go daily to astrologers
for forecasts about his health and safety.
Each morning, slip out early,
and listen at a neighbour's for the oracle.

Count each arc the sun drives through the sky,
and measure your lover's absence
by the slow drifting of the constellations.
Watch the moon wane and wax again,
envying him because he can see your beloved[6].

When you wake laughing from a dream,
you may take it as a sign
that you will soon be re-united with your lover;
but when nightmares torment you,
offer *pujas*, and meditate for peace of mind.

When he returns, offer a *puja* to Kama,
and worship in all the temples.
Go, with your friends, carrying the *purnapatra*[7]
covered with a shawl,
and distribute gifts to the poor and sick.

Feast the crows who were your messengers
on rice balls and sour rice gruel;
but, excepting this crowcraft, no acts of worship
should be performed until after
your lover has spent at least one night with you.

Once certain of his love, you may even speak
of becoming *sati*[8] when he dies;
but the *pujas*, *purnapatra* and other offerings
are too expensive to squander
on a man whose absence may have killed his love.

The besotted lover trusts you implicitly,
adapts himself to suit you,
does unhesitatingly whatever you ask,
never suspects your motives,
and thinks nothing of what he spends on you.

Vatsyayana has composed this chapter,
'Living as a Wife',
after studying various texts of Dattaka's[9] work.
What is not found here may be learned
by watching how other girls handle their lovers.

Who will ever understand the courtesan?
When love can be so deceptive
even in the hearts of virtuous women,
by what wisdom shall we establish
whether or not a courtesan truly loves a man?

True, by nature she is devious and greedy,
but those who court her tend already
to be well-advanced along the road to bankruptcy.
Does her lover attract or repel her?
Does it matter? Either way she'll bleed him dry.

---

5. The string of beads a bridegroom ties around the bride's neck during the wedding ceremony. It is meant to be worn as long as the husband lives. Presumably she had new *mangala* beads from each new lover.

6. The moon, Chandra, is masculine in Hindu mythology.

7. A large cup which was filled with offerings to be given to a temple, or distributed in thanks for having received good news.

8. The custom whereby a widow burns herself on her husband's funeral pyre. It was rare in ancient times, although mentioned in both epics. *Sati* was almost obligatory for queens of various Rajput ruling families and some old palaces have *sati* gates where the palmprints of the women who went to burn with their husbands' corpses can still be seen. The *Jauhar* was a mass-*sati* performed when a hopelessly beleaguered fortress could no longer withstand the enemy. The brooding fort of Chittorgarh saw three such mass immolations.

9. See Glossary

A girl and her attendants crowd into her lover's house. Perhaps, like the unfaithful courtesan of *Kama Sutra*, she has come to protest her devotion to him, with her maids adding vociferous support. The man, perhaps modelled on a sikh prince, sits austerely clad in white and listens unmoved. This painting, with its unusual use of colour, has a rare, jewel-like quality. *Basohli, early eighteenth century*

HOW TO MILK A WEALTHY LOVER

Your fee for one night should reflect
the custom of the country[1],
the time of year, the area in which you live,
your beauty and accomplishments
and the fees of your rivals.

The sages advise taking many lovers
so that they compete for favour,
each man bettering the last one's offer.
Spread your net wide:
catching new lovers can only make you wealthy.

Vatsyayana thinks you should always prefer
the man who pays in gold coin,
since coins once given are difficult to reclaim
and gold is the measure of all things –
even gemstones don't hold their value as well.

After coins, the following are acceptable,
in strict order of value:
gold, silver, copper, bronze and iron ingots,
pots and vessels in these metals,
bronze and iron tools, a wooden bedstead.

Next come quilts and blankets,
clothes of silk and linen,
sandalwood paste, perfumes and medicines,
black chillies, clay pitchers,
ghee[2], oil, wheat, barley, rice and livestock.

If you wish to take a lover for more
than your stated nightly fee,
you have an option: you can either accept
whatever he may choose to give you,
or you can scheme actively to fleece him.

The sages have said that if your lover
parts with his money freely,
and is generous enough to satisfy your needs,
you should be content with this,
and not resort to tricks or stratagems.

But Vatsyayana replies that if you earn
so much money without effort,
a little cunning will enable you
to double the amount at least,
and without arousing his slightest suspicions.

For instance, you can pledge your jewels
against debts incurred buying
gold and silver trinkets, jalebis and laddus[3],
corn, silks, cottons and wools,
perfumes, flowers, paan, supari[4] and so forth.

On the day when these payments fall due,
make sure your lover hears you
begging the tradesmen not to sell your jewels:
he will offer to lend you the money,
thus redeeming the jewels and paying your debts.

Constantly congratulate him on his wealth,
remembering your unfulfilled vow
to perform an important sacrifice, endow a temple,
plant a garden or grove, dig a step-well,
send gifts to a friend, or hold a garden-party.

Or go, sobbing and dishevelled, to his house
and say: 'I was on my way to see you
when I was attacked by a band of hooligans
(or, ad lib, the king's guard)
who threatened me and stole all my jewelry!'

Or tell him that your house caught fire,
or thieves dug through the wall
and rifled the strongroom of everything,
or that 'mother's' carelessness
has finally caught up with her, and ruined you.

If you can make him believe that the jewels
he had given you for safekeeping
have been lost along with everything else,
he will not think to ask for them
when, inevitably, your affair comes to an end.

You should run up debts on his behalf
and on transport to his house.
Make sure he's within earshot when 'mother'
starts kicking up a mighty fuss
about the amount of money he's costing you.

When he invites you to his friend's party
beg him not to insist, because
you have nothing to take as a gift.
If he offers to supply one,
remind him of his friend's great generosity.

---

1. Pali literature records that the courtesan Addhakasi was able, by leaving Benares and going to Rajagriha, to charge 1,000 panas a night and 500 panas a day. See p. 174, note 1.

2. See p. 118, note 11

3. Jalebis are made by piping concentric rings of dough into very hot fat and, when deep fried, steeping them in syrup. Laddus are round sweets made with sugar and various flavours. See p. 102, note 2.

4. See p. 138, note 6

A Jaipuri dancer of the eighteenth century, perhaps of the court
of Maharaja Jai Singh. Towards the end of his reign Jai Singh
spent a great deal of time drinking with concubines. One letter
to Maharaja Abhai Singh of Jodhpur, composed when he was
drunk, actually caused a war. In the end he issued an edict
forbidding anyone to approach him on business when he was
drunk. After Jai Singh's death, his famous library was given to a
courtesan, who distributed its precious manuscripts among her
low-born relatives. *Jaipur, eighteenth century*

Tell him you have sold your jewelry,
and that even the daily *puja*[5]
is a luxury you can no longer afford.
Engage craftsmen to work for you,
and have them send the bills to your lover.

By doing intimate little favours for people
like doctors and royal ministers,
you can persuade them to introduce you
to any number of wealthy men
who can afford to indulge your extravagance.

If a relative or friend of your lover
has fallen on hard times
you should, on your own initiative,
help with gifts and money –
this generosity will repay itself with interest.

Tell your lover that you need his help
to have your house repaired,
to celebrate the birth, to friends, of a son,
or simply to satisfy the bizarre
cravings that seize you during pregnancy.

You could pretend to be seriously ill
and unable to pay a doctor,
or to have got yourself into bad trouble
from which, you are afraid,
only his generosity can now extricate you.

Heap together your favourite jewels,
your copper pots and pans,
and your fine silks, then ask your lover to leave,
saying it would be embarrassing
for the pawnbroker to arrive and find him there.

Say you must immediately hire a smith
to enlarge your cooking pots,
because when your maids take them to the well,
the maids of other courtesans
have the impudence to claim that they are theirs.

You should constantly be thanking him
for his past generosity to you,
while letting your servants keep him informed
about how well other girls
are being looked after by their lovers.

When you are sitting, with your lover,
in the company of other women,
always exaggerate his wealth and generosity –
allow him to catch you blushing
and realize that you're lying to save his face.

Continue by remarking that a former lover,
whom you once sent packing,
has just made you a new and very liberal offer,
but that, of course, you have refused
out of love for the gentleman seated beside you.

Arrange for your lover to be present
to hear you screaming at 'mother'
when that old lady, in one of her frightful tempers,
starts insisting that you leave him
for a man who would be more generous to you.

When it is obvious that the affair is dead
and that he will not come again,
you must whimper, pouting like a little girl
and demanding obstinately that he
settle your fees, as he is now forsaking you.

---

5. See p. 116, note 3

This delightful miniature was painted to illustrate the *Rasikapriya* of Keshavdas, a poem heavily influenced by *Kama Sutra*. Lovers enter the very bedroom described by Vatsyayana, with its *vina* hanging from an ivory peg. The artist has added a bow and quiver of arrows. The carved head of Indra's white elephant Airavata guards the portico. *Malwa, c.1680*

THE END OF THE AFFAIR

You must watch constantly for signs
like frowning, or sulking,
which indicate that your lover is tiring of you.
A clear signal is when he will not pay
one *dinar*[1] more or less than your agreed fee.

He becomes friendly with your rivals,
no longer does as you ask
and, instead, behaves in a contrary manner.
In your presence he will not speak
to friends, but uses riddles and gestures.

He curtails even the charitable works
that were begun in your name
and, when you remind him of his promises,
affects surprise, saying:
'I don't recall promising you any such thing.'

He breaks an appointment with you,
saying he has urgent work to do for a friend,
but you know he spent the night
with another girl, because
her servants told your servants.

Conceal your knowledge of the fact
that he no longer loves you,
and use what time you have, while he is still
congratulating himself, to expropriate
everything of his you can lay your hands on.

With the connivance of an old creditor,
arrange for his gold and goods
to be impounded and sold to clear your debts;
if he angrily demands their return,
suggest he prove his claim in a court of law.

How to Get Rid of an Unwanted Lover
Be particularly charming to people he loathes;
do anything you can think of
that is calculated to annoy and upset him;
pout sulkily when he appears,
and stamp your ankleted feet in irritation.

Talk expansively of subjects about which
your lover is quite ignorant,
and refuse to acknowledge his flashes of wit;
criticize him whenever you can,
and humble him by mixing with his superiors.

Lose no opportunity to demonstrate
your cool indifference;
launch contemptuous tirades against a man
who has exactly the same faults;
snub him, and cultivate long, awkward silences.

When you're in bed with him, push aside
his gifts of *paan* and perfumes, don't let him
kiss your mouth, or touch your thighs,
become angry with him for having
marked your body with his nails and teeth.

When he tries to embrace you, fold
your arms across your breasts,
lie so stiff and still that he can scarcely
move your limbs and, finally,
cross one thigh firmly over the other.

When he says he wants to make love,
reply that you're too sleepy,
but if he insists, start jeering at him
when his orgasm is imminent:
'What? Surely not already? So little stamina?'

When, despite his desperate efforts,
he can no longer continue,
clap your hands ironically and praise his control;
but if he's strong and passionate,
lie silent, sad and motionless beneath him.

If he wants to make love during the day
say he has the lust of an ass[2];
lead him on for a while then get up abruptly
and leave the bedroom, saying
you've an appointment with some eminent man.

Be just as insulting outside the bedroom –
make sly remarks about him
when you're in company, ignore his jokes,
but laugh when he's being serious,
winking at your servants and musicians.

Listen attentively when he is speaking,
and then interrupt him with
some trivial, utterly unrelated observation;
criticize his voice and features;
be unwontedly tactless with his confidences.

No longer make him welcome when he calls;
ask for gifts he cannot afford
and, when you're tired of toying with him,
call two strong male servants
and order them to throw him out by force.

These four simple rules will make your fortune –
first investigate the man thoroughly,
next make him fall desperately in love with you,
then bleed him of his wealth
and, finally, throw him out when he is penniless.

---

1. The gold *dinar* of the Kushana and early Gupta kings was based on the Roman *denarius* and was of 124 grains. The silver *rupaka* of the Guptas (from which the modern *rupee* is descended) weighed 32–36 grains. The ancient silver *panas* which the courtesan Addhakasi (see p. 170, note 1) received in payment weighed 57.8 grains.

2. Shastri, in his Hindi commentary, uses the delightful expression *kama-gardabha* (Love Donkey).

An angry woman walks out on her lover, who is trying vainly
to placate her. This is another of the lovely paintings from the
Amarushataka, the amours of the poet-king Amaru, who wrote
(the translation is John Brough's): 'She neither turned away,
nor yet began to speak harsh words, nor did she bar the door;
but looked at him who was her love before as if he were an
ordinary man.' *Malwa, c.1680*

BOOK VII

APHRODISIACS AND SPELLS

LOVE POTIONS AND SEX AIDS

Kama Sutra is now complete.
If its teachings
bring you no happiness in love,
you must turn to
Atharva Veda[1] and other magical texts.

A lack of beauty, presence, youth
or liberality –
the qualities that make a man desirable –
may often be countered
by the spells and recipes of the grimoires.

To Make Yourself Beautiful
Ointment made from the leaves
of rosebay,
the fragrant costus shrub
and the dwarf plum
will increase beauty one hundredfold.

If you steep a cotton wick
in the powdered leaves of these plants,
and burn it in myrobalan oil
held in a human skull,
it produces the most bewitching eyeshadow.

Oil of acanthus, sarsaparilla,
hogweed, floss flower
and blue lotus, or even a garland
of their petals,
will greatly enhance your charm.

A small bone from a peacock
or hyena, sealed by
an astrologer into a pure gold amulet
and worn on the right wrist,
will have the same mysterious effect.

So too a wrinkled jujube berry
tied around the wrist,
or a conch shell chased in gold
and consecrated with
the *dharana-yogas*[2] of *Atharva Veda*.

To Enslave a Lover
Anoint your penis, before lovemaking,
with honey into which
you have powdered black pepper,
long pepper and *datura*[3] –
it will utterly devastate your lady.

Leaves caught as they fall from trees
and powdered with peacock-bone
and fragments of a corpse's winding-sheet
will, when dusted lightly
on the penis, bewitch any woman living.

If you crush milky chunks of cactus
with sulphur and realgar,
dry the mixture seven times, powder it
and apply it to your penis,
you'll satisfy the most demanding lover.

And if, to these powerful ingredients,
you add a monkey's turd,
grind them together and sprinkle the powder
on your unsuspecting lover's head,
she will be your devoted slave for life.

If, like the Nagas[4], you place slivers
of catechu wood steeped
in mango-oil under the bark of an aromatic tree,
you will, six months later,
have a perfume as fragrant as that tree's.

If you dip camel bones in eclipta juice
and burn them for collyrium,
keep the collyrium in a camel-bone pot
and apply it with a brush tipped
with camel hair, it makes the eyes most beautiful.

To Increase Potency[5]
Honey-sweetened milk in which
the testicles of a ram
or a goat have been simmered
has the effect, when drunk,
of making a man as powerful as a bull.

Pumpkin seeds ground with almonds
and sugarcane root,
or with cowhage root and strips of bamboo,
and stirred into honeyed milk,
have the same arousing effect.

The sages say that wheat-flour cakes
baked with honey and sugar
and sprinkled with the powdered seeds
of pumpkin and cowhage
give one strength for a thousand women.

---

1. See Glossary

2. *Yogic* exercises involving deep concentration.

3. The green thorn apple. All parts of the weed are strongly intoxicant, narcotic and aphrodisiac with properties similar to those of deadly nightshade.

4. See Glossary

5. There is a *paan-wallah* who sits in his cubby-hole just opposite Chowpatti Beach in Bombay selling what he describes as a *palang-tod* (bed-breaker) of a *paan*. Exactly what goes into the leaf with the smear of lime, crushed areca nuts and spices is not quite clear, but whatever it is, it has made him a fortune.

The prince and princess make love in the *Sthita* posture. Behind them on the bed lie
a garland of yellow amaranth, a box of *paans*, flasks perhaps containing wine or an
aphrodisiac potion, and a Chinese vase, possibly filled with sandalwood ointment.
Potions containing opium were commonly used in Rajasthan. The peacock was a
symbol of love, which is why its bones were used in various enchantments.
Rajasthani, eighteenth century (detail)

The yolk of a single sparrow's egg
stirred into rice pudding
that has been thickened with cream,
wild-honey and *ghee*[6]
has the same invigorating effect.

Shelled black-sesame seeds, steeped
in the yolk of sparrows' eggs
and ground with water-chestnut, nut grass,
cowhage, wheat and gram into milky,
honey-sweetened porridge are very efficacious.

If you mix two ounces each of *ghee*,
honey, sugar and *mahwa*[7] flowers
with a quarter ounce of liquorice
and a quart of milk,
you have made the nectar of *yogis*.

To Cope with Impotence
A man who climaxes too swiftly
should arouse his lady
by caressing her clitoris with his fingers
and flooding the well
of her *yoni* before he enters her.

If, during lovemaking, the erection
cannot be sustained because
the man is old, or simply exhausted,
he should use the delicate
oral techniques given in an earlier chapter.

The man who is utterly unable
to achieve an erection
should pleasure his wife with a phallus
crafted from materials like
gold, silver, copper, iron, ivory or horn.

Babhravya's followers will tell you
that phalloi of lead and tin
are smoothest, coolest and most rewarding,
but Vatsyayana recommends that you experiment:
it may even be that wood will satisfy her.

The artificial phallus should be shaped
to your natural proportions.
It will be more arousing for the lady
if the outside is studded
with a profusion of large, smooth nodules.

Those fashioned from two locking rings
are easiest to put on
and to remove afterwards; some are even made
in three sections, presumably
for men who need to vary their proportions.

The simplest of all is a single
strip of lead which winds
tightly around the shaft of the penis.
The most sophisticated ties on
round the waist and accommodates the testicles.

If a properly crafted phallus
is quite beyond your means,
smooth a snake gourd or hollow a bamboo,
steep it in antiseptic oils,
and fasten it by a thong about your waist.

Large round seeds or wooden beads
may also be smoothed,
strung on a thong, carefully oiled,
wound around the penis
and used as an inexpensive substitute.

Perforating the Penis[8]
Just as in our northern countries
it is common for people
to have their daughters' ears pierced,
so the peoples of the south
customarily perforate their sons' penises.

A grown man who wishes to perform
this operation on himself
takes a very sharp needle and, pulling
the foreskin forward, pierces
it obliquely, taking care to avoid the veins.

He keeps the wound immersed in water
for as long as bleeding persists,
but if he wishes to enlarge the holes
he has vigorous intercourse
not once, but several times that night.

Daily for five days he will bathe
the wounds in antiseptics made from pennywort,
purging cassia, oleander, conchflower
and Arabian jasmine –
the five great purifying lotions.

---

6. See p. 118, note 11

7. *Madhuca longfolia macbride*, more commonly known as the Mowra Butter Tree. The wild hill-tribes of the Western Ghats make a liqueur from *mahwa* flowers by fermenting them with wild honey and a strip of mango bark in natural volcanic potholes in the rocks, sealing these with a mixture of straw, clay and cowdung and leaving them for six months. The resultant liqueur is said to be very fragrant and delicious.

8. Vatsyayana himself makes it clear that this custom was not prevalent in his own, northern Indian society. Probably he was reporting gossip, and the operation sounds very dangerous as it is described.

A lady of the doe type applies an unguent which will help her to accommodate her impatiently waiting lover (see p. 182). The aromatic, oleo-resinous gum of the *sal* tree is still used as an aphrodisiac, given in 20-grain doses in a pint of milk. The powdered resin is used, in Ayurvedic medicine, to relax the delicate mucous membranes of the throat and the female genitals. The root of the Indian madder is used to remove obstruction in urinary passages and to reduce inflammation and swelling. *Mewar, c.1760*

He will enlarge the holes gradually,
using first thin stems of cane,
then thicker ones and, finally, winding
sturdy strips of lead through
and twisting them into heavy rings.

Meanwhile he will be cleaning
the wounds and helping
them heal with daily dressings of honey
and liquorice powder, and by
bathing them frequently in oil of cashew.

When the holes are completely healed,
fully opened, and no longer hurt,
the man will insert penis-rings made of bone,
clay, stone or wood,
choosing from the vast array available.

Long, rounded, flattened at each end;
shaped like mortars, flowers,
birds' feet, thorny cucumbers, elephants' trunks;
octagonal, wheel-shaped, triangular;
smooth or rough: there is no end to their variety[9].

Enlarging the Penis or Yoni
First rub your penis with wasp stings
and massage it with sweet oil.
When it swells, let it dangle for ten nights
through a hole in your bed,
going to sleep each night on your stomach.

After this period use a cool ointment
to remove the pain and swelling.
By this method men like *vitas*[10], of insatiable
sexual appetite, manage to keep
their penises enlarged throughout their lives.

Winter cherry, a root of the Lodh tree,
nightshade berries and a jellyfish,
when crushed into buffalo butter, cactus milk
or great-leaved-caladium juice,
will swell a man's penis for one month.

To keep the swelling for six months,
massage your penis with oil
that has been very slowly extracted from seeds
of watermelon and pomegranate,
khus khus[11] grass and deadly nightshade berries.

By applying an ointment made from
crushed barleria leaves
to her *yoni*, the elephant woman
can spend at least one night
discovering the delights of being a doe.

Likewise the doe can use honey
mixed with powdered roots
of lotus, madder, *sal*[12], the blue lotus
and the mongoose plant
to accommodate a stallion for one night.

Miscellaneous Recipes and Charms
To deter a man, a lady may apply
ointment of *babchi*[13] seed,
bay berry, black plum, purging cassia,
eclipta, cactus and iron filings –
nothing withers a penis faster.

A trick that will turn
the reddest lips dead white is to paint them
with lac steeped seven times
in the sweat scraped
from the testicle of a white stallion.

The juice of black hellebore,
tellicherry bark,
henna, the butterfly pea
or the betel nut
will quickly redden them again.

A flute dipped into a potion
of costus, rosebay, mint and silver fir,
spurge cactus and red cedar,
will cause any girl
who hears it to become the flautist's slave.

Spells for increasing beauty, for potency
and for satisfying women
may be found in *Atharva Veda* and the *tantras*[14].
but always first consult a *brahmin*
skilled in the *Veda* and these magical texts.

Do not use recipes that harm your body,
that require you to kill a bird or animal
or to use impure, disgusting substances.
Choose only those recipes
which *brahmins* or trusted friends recommend.

---

9. The fifteenth-century traveller Nicolo de Conti reported that old women used to sell tiny bells of gold, silver and copper to be sewn into the foreskin. Some young men had as many as a dozen of these bells and the sound of jingling, as they walked, was considered honourable.

10. See p. 32, including note 14

11. See p. 110, note 4

12. See p. 46, note 3

13. *Psoralea corylifolia* The seeds, at least, have aphrodisiac properties imputed to them.

14. See Glossary

The sound of Krishna's flute entices Radha deeper and deeper into the forest. It used also to charm the village girls whom he led in moonlit dances when their husbands were asleep. The recipe given opposite no doubt harks back to these legends.

The iconography of the magic flute appears again in the medieval tale of Sohini and Mahinwal, a favourite theme with painters. Mahinwal is always shown playing his flute on the far bank of a river across which Sohini, entranced by the music, swims with the aid of an upturned clay pot. *Basohli, c.1710*

VATSYAYANA'S BLESSING

After collecting and studying the works
of the great masters of love,
and testing the accuracy of their contents,
this *Kama Sutra* was composed
as a slender summary of the science of love.

If you have grasped the essence of this work,
you will never permit desire
or your emotions to prevent you following
Dharma, *Artha* and *Kama*,
your own conscience and the laws of society.

Kama Sutra chronicles all sexual practice,
the natural with the corrupt,
but each *sutra* must be understood in context:
the writer has taken trouble to indicate
which techniques should be condemned.

A work such as this must be useful
to men and women of many different nations.
Not all techniques will suit everyone:
abstract and use, therefore,
only what is natural in your own country.

Having studied the extensive poetics
of Babhravya's seven disciples
and all other available literature on this subject,
Vatsyayana has composed in *sutras*[1],
to elevate the study of love to a science.

Vatsyayana wrote this *Kama Sutra*
while a celibate *yogi*
who had already attained undisturbed *samadhi*[2];
not from any impure motive,
but to guide the people on their pilgrimage.

Only by grasping the essence of *Kama Sutra*
and rooting every act in *Dharma*
can you enjoy the fruit of *Artha* and *Kama*,
learn to live happily with others
and, finally, quiet the senses and find peace.

If you are wise and use this *Kama Sutra*
with *Dharma* and *Artha* ever in view,
neither moved by passion nor swayed by desire,
you will know perfect happiness –
this is my promise.

---

1. See Introduction for a discussion of the *sutra*, or aphoristic, style.

2. The eighth and final stage of *yoga* in Patanjali's *Yoga Sutra* is enlightenment – the highest spiritual achievement for a Hindu.

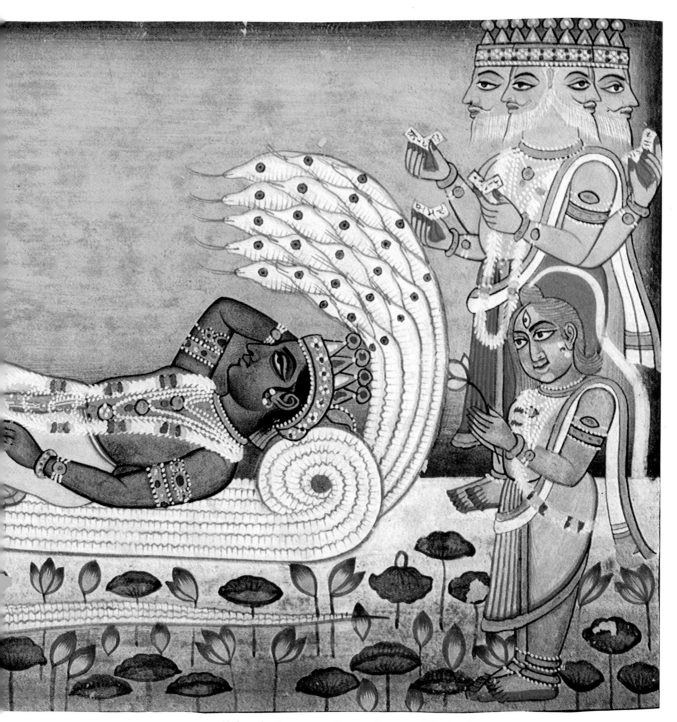

Vishnu the Preserver reclines on the serpent Shesha, the
symbol of eternity. Vishnu embodies *Dharma*, the self-existent,
all-pervading power which preserves and upholds the
universe. He is attended by his wife Laxmi, goddess of wealth
and source of *Artha*. Nearby stands Shiva the Destroyer, who as
the *linga* personifies both *Kama* and its control. At top right is
Brahma the Creator, the highest reality, in whom the three aims
are reconciled and transcended in *Moksha* or salvation, the state
which the enlightened *yogi*, represented here by the
worshipping *brahmin* at lower left, attains by perfect balance
and control. *Rajasthani, eighteenth century*

GLOSSARY

Abhira King of Kotta, in what is now Gujerat state. He was killed by a washerman hired by Vasumitra's outraged brother.

Ahalya Wife of the sage Gotama, she committed adultery with the god Indra, who came to her in Gotama's form. Gotama turned her into a pillar of stone.

Ambapali The famous courtesan of Vaishali. The Buddha, passing through the city on his last journey, declined a civic reception offered by the city elders in favour of her dinner invitation.

Ananga Ranga This love text was composed by the poet Kalyana Malla for a prince of the Lodi family. Probably sixteenth century.

Andhra Modern Andhra Pradesh, virtually identical with the former realm of the Nizam of Hyderabad. In Vatsyayana's time it was ruled by the Shatavahana dynasty.

Anga A small kingdom on the borders of Bengal. Its capital, Champa, on the river Ganga, was a port of considerable importance.

Aparantaka A region of the northern Konkan, approximating to modern Goa. In the first century AD, its coasts harboured pirates who raided the ships carrying gold, spices and ivory to the Roman empire.

Arjuna Hero of the *Mahabharata* and of the *Bhagavad Gita*. He abducted Subhadra, Princess of Dvaraka, in his chariot. She acted as his charioteer and drove him to safety through her father's army.

Aryans The Indo-European tribes which entered northern India and Iran from the steppes of Central Asia in about the fifteenth century BC. By Vatsyayana's day they were well established throughout northern and central India.

Asvins Twin gods, equivalents of the Greek Dioskouri. They accompanied the sun god in his fiery three-wheeled chariot and were physicians to the gods of Indra's heaven. Among their good deeds, were rescuing shipwrecked mariners, providing artificial legs for the maimed and finding husbands for old maids.

Atharva Veda The fourth of the holy books of the Aryans. It consists mainly of magical spells and verse incantations and is later than *Rig Veda* and *Yajur Veda*.

Auddalaki The patronymic of Svetaketu.

Babhravya This sage condensed Svetaketu's love teachings to a mere one hundred and fifty chapters some time in the fifth century BC, or earlier, creating the sixty-fourfold division of the lovemaking techniques in imitation of the structure of *Rig Veda*.

Babhravyakarika The title of Babhravya's great seven-part work. It survived into the middle ages, for Yashodhara quotes from it.

Bali A demon who accumulated enough power, through sacrifice and penance, to turn the gods out of their kingdom. Vishnu tricked him into losing it again by assuming the form of a dwarf and asking him for as much ground as he could cover in three strides. Vishnu's first two strides covered heaven and earth. Bali was allowed to keep the nether regions.

Balkh A province in northern Afghanistan, lying between the Hindukush mountains and the Oxus river. In Vatsyayana's day it was ruled by the Kushanas, whom the Aryans regarded as barbarians.

Banga The rich lands of modern Bangladesh which adjoined the Gupta empire. They were annexed by Samudragupta.

Brahma One of the three gods of later Hinduism, he was identified with Prajapati, the Creator. Today the only prominent Brahma temple left in India is at Pushkar, near Ajmer.

Brihaspati He began his career as a Vedic god, but was later demoted to a sage, performing the duties of high priest in Indra's heaven. He is said to be the source of the *Artha* teachings, and hence a forerunner of Kautilya.

Buddha Gautama, born a prince of the Sakya tribe in about 563 BC. He lived in luxury until the age of twenty-six when, disgusted by the poverty around him, he renounced the world. He is said to have attained enlightenment six years later. By Vatsyayana's day Buddhism was on the decline in India.

Charayana The Mauryan sage who expounded the first section of Babhravya's seven-part work. He is mentioned in the *Arthashastra* of Kautilya.

Charvaka A founder of the atheist, materialist schools known as Lokayatas. Their philosophy is summed up in the verse: 'As long as he lives a man should live happily and drink *ghee*, though he run into debt; for when the body is turned to ashes how can there be any return to life?'

Chola A Dravidian kingdom in the region of modern Madras. Traders from this region were responsible for the spread of Hinduism to the Indonesian archipelago.

Damayanti A legendary princess whose story is told in *Mahabharata*. She chose her own husband, King Nala, who later lost both her and his kingdom at a gambling tournament. They were reunited and regained their throne after many years of separation.

Dandakya King of the Bhojas, a people whose country lay to the south of the Vindhya mountains. While out hunting he saw a *brahmin* girl in the forest and, overcome by lust, raped her. Her father laid a curse upon him and destroyed him, his family and every living thing in his kingdom under a thick rain of dust.

Dattaka The sage who was approached by Virasena, chief of the courtesans of Pataliputra, to lecture them on the sixth part of Babhravya's work. He was said to have been turned into a woman after polluting a rite of Shiva and to have experienced lovemaking with both sexes. A fragmentary metrical resume of his work has apparently recently been unearthed.

Draupadi The heroine of the *Mahabharata* and polyandrous wife to the five Pandava brothers. Arjuna won her in an archery contest in which he defeated the assembled kings and princes of India. It was during the exile of the Pandavas that she was insulted by Kichaka.

Dushyanta The king who, while out hunting, fell in love with Shakuntala, the daughter of the sage Kanva, and married her according to the *Gandharva* rite. The story of their love affair is the subject of Kalidasa's greatest play, the *Abhijnana Shakuntala*.

Ganesha One of the most popular Hindu gods, he is the remover of obstacles and is usually represented as a short, pot-bellied man with four arms and a single-tusked elephant's head. His festival is celebrated with particular enthusiasm in Bombay, which comes to a standstill as processions of worshippers follow trucks bearing huge clay images of the god down to Chowpatti beach, where they are carried out to sea and then immersed.

Gauda A kingdom that coincides roughly with the modern Murshirabad district of West Bengal. Its people were great seafarers.

Ghotakamukha A Mauryan sage also referred to in Kautilya's *Arthashastra*. He taught the third section of Babhravya's work.

Gonardiya He wrote on the fourth section of *Babhravyakarika*. He is mentioned in the *Mahabhashya*, Patanjali's commentary on the *sutras* of Panini the grammarian.

Gonikaputra He expounded the fifth section of Babhravya's work, and is also mentioned in Patanjali's *Mahabhashya*.

Gotama A sage, descended from the noble *rishi* Angirases, whose wife Ahalya was seduced by Indra. He is credited with being the author of *Rig Veda*, I: 74f-93.

Himalaya Literally 'home of ice'. The mountain kingdoms of Kashmir and modern Himachal Pradesh were in Vatsyayana's day under the rule of Bactrian Greeks.

Indra The king of the Vedic pantheon, he wields a thunderbolt, is addicted to the intoxicating *soma* juice and to beautiful women, especially, it seems, if married to holy sages. He rides the white elephant, Airavata.

Indrani Wife of Indra and voluptuous daughter of the demon Puloman, whom Indra slew.

Kalinga A country which comprised much of modern Orissa. It was the scene of the Mauryan emperor Ashoka's greatest victory, in 261 BC. The slaughter which left Kalinga defenceless was so horrible that even Ashoka was sickened, and turned to Buddhism, which became the religion of the Mauryan empire.

Kalyana Malla The author of *Ananga Ranga*.

Kama The Hindu god of love. According to some schools he is the oldest god of all, having inspired Creation itself. In later Hinduism he is a frivolous young man, riding a parrot, carrying a bow of sugarcane strung with humming bees. He carries five arrows tipped with lotus flowers.

Kashi Modern Varanasi (British Benares), the city of Shiva which was first mentioned in Vedic times. Damodara Gupta called it 'the ornament of the whole earth' and compared it to Indra's city Amaravati. In Gupta times it was a centre of Vedic studies, and it is quite likely to have been the city in which *Kama Sutra* was composed. It is the holiest Hindu city and the crowds that flock to its bathing *ghats* on the Ganga are, if anything, growing vaster each year.

Kaulas A left-hand *tantric* sect which used ritualized sexual intercourse as part of its worship. The preparations for the ritual included meditation, using *mantra* and *yantra*, *hatha-yoga* and breathing exercises. The Kaulas cloaked themselves in secrecy and deterred curiosity by publishing verses like that quoted by Tarkalamkara in his commentary on the *Mahanirvana Tantra*: 'Who thrusts his penis into his mother's womb and massages her breasts and places his foot on his *guru's* head will not experience rebirth.'

Kharvata An ancient city whose location has been lost.

Kichaka The commander-in-chief of the army of King Virata, in whose court the disguised Pandavas took refuge during their exile. Kichaka's legendary strength was matched only by his arrogance. When Draupadi spurned his advances he kicked her in front of the assembled court. For this insult Bhima killed him and reduced his body to shapeless pulp.

Kotta The kingdom of Abhira, part of modern Gujerat.

Krishna The best loved of all Indian gods, and the eighth incarnation of Vishnu. In *Mahabharata* he serves as Arjuna's charioteer and delivers the battlefield sermon that became *Bhagavad Gita*. His cult centred on Vrindavan, on the banks of the Yamuna, where he spent his time playing his flute and enticing the village girls to dance with him in the moonlight. His love affair with Radha is the subject of *Gita Govinda* and other famous poems.

Kuchumara The last of Babhravya's seven scholiasts. His work, which dealt with sexual aids, aphrodisiacs, spells and *mantras*, was known as *Kuchumaratantra*.

Kurangi The love affair between this princess and an untouchable who turns out to be a prince forms the basis of *Avimaraka*, an early Sanskrit play which may have been composed by Bhasa. In the play, the sage Narada himself comes down from heaven to bless the couple and approve their marriage by the *Gandharva* rite.

Lat A region of what is modern Gujerat. In Vatsyayana's time it was probably under the rule, or overlordship, of the Indo-Scythian Shakas.

Laxmi Originally the daughter of the sage Bhrigu. As a goddess she is the wife of Vishnu and was reincarnated both as Sita and as Radha. She is the goddess of wealth and fortune, but worshipped on her own she becomes the mother of all things, the *shakti* or divine female energy.

Mahabharata The first of the great Hindu epics. It was composed by Vyasa, who dictated it to Ganesha, and tells the story of the feuding Pandava and Kaurava cousins, and their final reckoning in the battle of Kurukshetra, which is thought to have been fought between 1400 and 1000 BC. The 100,000 couplets of the present text did not reach their final form until about 400 BC.

Mallanaga The author of *Kama Sutra*. Vatsyayana was his clan name.

Manu The First Man, who in Hindu mythology combines the roles of Adam and Noah. He too built an ark to survive a great flood, and was beached on a mountaintop. He is said to be the first human teacher of the *Dharma* wisdom, but the *Dharmashastra* which bears his name did not reach its final form until the second or third century AD.

Muladeva A shadowy figure credited with being the first teacher of sorcery, sleight-of-hand and deception. He sometimes appears as a master-thief, sometimes as a great magician, occasionally as a gambler. According to the Jain chronicler Devendra, he also wrote a treatise on the art of thieving, the *Steyashastra*, which is now lost.

Nagara A name sometimes used for Pataliputra, the capital city of the Guptas. But here it probably refers to another city, because when Vatsyayana wants to say Pataliputra he says it without equivocation (see p.18).

Nagas A group of hill tribes inhabiting the region between Assam and Burma. They were hostile to the Aryans and managed to preserve their independence until the nineteenth century.

Nandi The white bull who serves Shiva as a mount. In mythology he was the guardian at Shiva's gate and even today there is a carved white marble bull guarding the door of every Shiva temple.

Orissa An eastern state of modern India, and a centuries-old centre of erotic art. The thirteenth-century sun temple at Konarak and the temples at Bhubaneshwar are covered in amorous couples so exquisitely carved that the stone almost seems to be breathing. The region is a hotbed of *tantricism* and produced vast numbers of erotic palm-leaf manuscripts, called 'brides' books'.

Panchala The region which is now the Punjab. Draupadi, heroine of the *Mahabharata,* was a Panchala princess. The oldest traditions pinpoint this region as the source of the ancient love teachings. The first human teacher of *Kama* wisdom, Svetaketu, came from Panchala.

Panchasayaka Literally 'The Five Arrows', a love text composed early in the fourteenth century by Jyotirishvara Kavishekhara

Pandya The southernmost of the ancient Dravidian kingdoms, occupying the country to the north of *Kanyakumari* (Cape Comorin). The capital was the lovely city of Madurai.

Pashupati Shiva, worshipped as 'Lord of the Animals'. According to Basham, the horned ithyphallic god of the Indus Valley civilization may have been an early prototype.

Pataliputra Modern Patna. Founded in the fifth century BC by Ajatashatru of Magadha, it became the capital both of the Mauryan and Gupta empires. The Greek Ambassador Megasthenes, who spent several years at the court of Chandragupta Maurya said that 'even Susa and Ecbatana could not rival the beauty and grandeur of Pataliputra.' The Chinese traveller Fa Hsien, visiting the city seven hundred years later in the reign of the Gupta emperor Chandra Gupta II, said: 'the royal palace and the halls, the walls and the gates with the inlaid sculpture work seem to be the work of superhuman spirits.' The city was destroyed by fire in about AD 600.

Pattana An ancient city whose location has been forgotten.

Prachya A general name for the eastern countries, which included Anga, Banga, Gauda and Kalinga. The regions singled out for criticism by Vatsyayana usually lie on the borders of the Aryan world.

Prajapati The Creator, later identified with Brahma. When he awoke in the primordial waters he found himself alone and wept, creating the air, earth and sky from his tears. A beautiful hymn in *Rig Veda* (X: 90) has another version, where Prajapati offers himself as the first sacrifice and wild animals, hymns and chants, sacrificial spells, horses, cattle, goats and sheep, priests, warriors, merchants and serfs spring from his dismembered body.

Ramayana The second of the great Hindu epics, credited to the sage Valmiki and probably completed some time around 300 BC. It tells of the exile of Rama and Sita, the abduction of Sita by the *rakshasa* king Ravana and the war in which Rama, aided by the monkey god-king Hanuman, won her back.

Ratikallolini An obscure love text composed by one Dikshita Samaraja. The name means 'River of Love'. It seems to be a late work.

Ratimanjari A miniature love text of only sixty verses, composed by Jayadeva between the fourteenth and sixteenth centuries. It was synthesized from *Smaradipika*.

Ratirahasya After *Kama Sutra*, the most famous of the love texts, written perhaps as early as the eleventh century by a Pandit Kokkoka. It is often called *Koka Shastra*, 'Koka's Book'. It follows *Kama Sutra* closely, but the section on *sattvas*, or women's natures, is lifted from *Natyashastra*. Originally these potted descriptions were intended to help actresses portray various kinds of women.

Ratiratnapradipika A love text said to have been composed by Maharaja Praudha Devaraya of Vijayanagara (ruled 1422–66). It contains the only complete account of cunnilingus techniques and also shows a great deal of *tantric* influence.

Ravana The demon king who is the villain of *Ramayana*. He is depicted with ten heads and twenty arms, each of which carries a sword, mace or other weapon.

Rig Veda The greatest of the *Vedas*, it is the oldest sacred book in the world still in use. Its collection of 1,028 hymns was composed between 1500 and 1200 BC as the nomadic Aryan tribes entered India. It is considered vital that not a syllable of this *sruti* (oral) scripture should be lost and *brahmin* boys throughout India still learn the entire text by heart, cross-checking through an elaborate system of stresses, notes and metres to ensure that every sound is in the right place. It is thus heard today exactly as it sounded three thousand years ago.

Sarasvati A goddess worshipped as a consort of Brahma and as a patroness of music, art and belles lettres. She is credited with the invention both of the Sanskrit language and the *devanagari* script.

Saurashtra The leaf-shaped peninsula jutting from Gujerat into the Arabian Sea. During Vatsyayana's lifetime it was probably ruled by the Shakas, but Chandra Gupta II annexed it to the Gupta empire.

Seven Rishis The seers who were translated to the skies as stars in the Great Bear were Kashyapa, Atri, Vasishta, Vishvamitra, Gotama, Jamadagni and Bharadwaja.

Shakas The building of the Great Wall of China by Ch'in Shih Huang Ti caused ripples of migration which pushed a group of Scythian tribes into Bactria and subsequently into the Greek kingdoms of northwest India. By the middle of the first century BC they had overrun the Greeks and by Vatsyayana's day they controlled Malwa, Gujerat and the country as far east as Mathura. The Aryans called them Shakas. In about AD 388 their capital, Ujjain, was captured and their lands annexed by Chandra Gupta II.

Shakuntala Daughter of the sage Kanva. See **Dushyanta**

Shatkarni The Shatavahana king who drove the Shakas out of Andhra in about AD 130. The mention of his name helps fix the earliest possible date for *Kama Sutra*.

Shiva One of the Hindu trinity. He is traditionally depicted as an ash-smeared *yogi*, his hair coiled upon his head, adorned by the crescent moon. He is at once destroyer and revivifier, ascetic and sensualist. As the consort of the great goddess Durga, or Kali, he is the erect *linga*, and is important in *tantra*. Music, yoga, dance, drama and the love teachings all find their source in him.

Sind A province now in Pakistan. In Vatsyayana's time it was part of the Sassanian empire, ruled however by Hindu chiefs who were feudatories of the Persian emperor.

Sita The daughter of King Janaka of Videha, and the heroine of the *Ramayana*, she is the Hindu model of the faithful wife.

Smaradipika A love text composed between the thirteenth and fifteenth centuries by one Sri Minanath, who claims to have consulted 'numerous *Kamashastras*'. It was the model for *Ratimanjari*.

Srngararasaprabandhadipika 'The Light of Love', composed by Harihara, lists sixty-four sexual postures, but the descriptions stop with *Garuda*, the thirty-sixth. It is of uncertain date.

Strirajya The name means 'kingdom of women'. It was a matriarchal state in the Himalayan northwest and is mentioned also in the *Markandeya Purana* (LVIII: 39) and *Mahabharata* (III: 54 and XII: 4). Megasthenes, Polyaenus and Solinus confirm tales of a women's realm in India. Its people were probably tribals who may perhaps be identified with the fair-skinned Madras of the *Mahabharata* of whom Karna says: 'they are non-Aryans born in a bad land, who know nothing of the holy laws.'

Subhadra The sister of Krishna and daughter of King Vasadeva of Dvaraka. See **Arjuna**

Suvarnanabha The Mauryan sage who expounded the second part of Babhravya's long text. His work was probably called *Ratinirnaya* ('An Investigation of Carnal Love').

Svetaketu Auddalaki A Vedic sage, son of Uddalaka Aruni and the first human teacher of the *Kama* wisdom. He is mentioned in the oldest *Upanishads* as having learned the sex mysteries from a scholar called Pravahana Jaivali.

Tantras Literally 'looms', they are a series of texts, some Shaivite, some Vaishnavite and the remainder belonging to the left-hand Shakta schools. See **Kaulas**. Shaktism was an amalgam of Shiva worship and the pre-Aryan mother-goddess cults, and it is this school that has come to be synonymous with the word *tantra*, although it claims less than half of the official texts. In essence all *tantras* use seed-*mantras* and *yantras*, or mystical diagrams, for meditation and their ultimate aim is identical with that of *yoga* – enlightenment and freedom from rebirth.

Uddalaka Aruni A Vedic sage who, in *Chandogya Upanishad*, gives his son Svetaketu the famous '*tat tvam asi*' ('That thou art') teaching.

Vatsagulmaka A state in the modern Akola district, lying between the Indhyadhri hills and the Godavari river. Vatsyayana refers to it as a 'southern' state, by which he means that it was on the southern fringe of Aryan India, in the northern Deccan. As Vatsagulmaka became an independent kingdom only after AD 320, Vatsyayana's specific references to its royal palace provide powerful evidence for the dating of *Kama Sutra* itself.

Vatsyayana Author of *Kama Sutra*. His first name was Mallanaga. His date is uncertain and little is known about him (see Introduction). Bandhu states that he was a Kashmiri *brahmin* from Kishtawar who ran away from home at the age of eleven, got his education at Varanasi and Pataliputra and wandered the length and breadth of the country gaining experience of the subject about which he was to write. The story sounds spurious and has possibly been confused with the story of the Kashmiri Pandit Kokkoka who wrote *Ratirahasya* and whose appetite for women was legendary. The first literary mention of Vatsyayana is in the fifth-century *Vasavadutta* of Subandhu: '[The mountain] was as rich in elephants and perfumed jungles as Mallanaga's *Kama Sutra* in the ways of delighting and enjoying mistresses.'

Vedas Collections of hymns and oblational verses dating from about 1,500 BC. *Rig Veda* contains nothing but hymns, *Yajur Veda* contains *mantras* and instructions for performing rituals, *Sama Veda* is a compilation of musical chants based on the *Rig Veda* hymns and *Atharva Veda* contains hymns, magic spells and incantations. Each *Veda* had, and still has, its own priesthood. They are the holiest Hindu texts.

Vidarbha A kingdom lying to the south of the Vindhya mountains, in the northern Deccan. It was the homeland of Princess Damayanti.

Yakshas The attendant spirits of Kubera, the dwarf god of wealth, and custodians of all treasure buried in the earth or in the roots of trees. The hero of Kalidasa's *Meghaduta* is a Yaksha banished from Kubera's Himalayan kingdom of Alaka.

BIBLIOGRAPHY

Sanskrit texts

PRAUDHA DEVARAYA. *Ratiratnapradipika*. Edited by Dhundiraj Shastri. Chaukamba Sanskrit Series, Varanasi. 1967

HARIHARA. *Srngararasaprabandhadipikamanjari*. Edited by Dhundiraj Shastri. Chaukamba Sanskrit Series, Varanasi. 1967

JAYADEVA. *Ratimanjari*. Edited by Dhundiraj Shastri. Chaukamba Sanskrit Series, Varanasi. 1967

Ratimanjari. Edited, with Hindi translation, by R. Dvivedi. Chaukamba Sanskrit Series, Varanasi. 1976

JYOTIRISHVARA KAVISHEKHARA. *Panchasayakam*. Edited by Dhundiraj Shastri. Chaukamba Sanskrit Series, Varanasi. 1967

KOKKOKA. *Ratirahasyam*. Edited by Jivanand Sharma. Bombay Sanskrit Series. 1925

KALYANA MALLA. *Ananga Ranga*. Edited by V. P. Bhandari. Chaukamba Sanskrit Series, Varanasi. 1923

Ananga Ranga. Edited, with Hindi translation, by Pandit Ramchandra Jha. Chaukamba Sanskrit Series, Varanasi. 1973

SRI MINANATHA. *Smaradipika*. Edited by Dhundiraj Shastri. Chaukamba Sanskrit Series, Varanasi. 1967

MATHURA PRASAD. *Ratikelikutuhalam*. Gopal Brothers, Delhi. 1954

NARAYANA PRASAD (Ed.). *Kokasaravaidyaka*. Khemraj Srikrishnadas, Bombay. 1960

DIKSHITA SAMARAJA. *Ratikallolini*. Edited by Dhundiraj Shastri. Chaukamba Sanskrit Series, Varanasi. 1967

THAKUR V. B. SINGH (Ed.). *Kamakalasara*. Hindi Sahitya Kutira, Varanesi. 1954

VATSYAYANA. *Kamasutram*. Ms. in Oriental Institute, Baroda. Seventeenth century

Kamasutram. Edited, with Hindi translation and commentary, by Devadutta Shastri. Chaukamba Sanskrit Series, Varanasi. 1964

Translations

V. C. BANDHU. *Kama Sutra*. Universal, New Delhi. 1973

J. BROUGH. *Poems from the Sanskrit*. Penguin, London. 1968

SIR RICHARD BURTON. *The Ananga Ranga of Kalyana Malla*. William Kimber, London. 1963

The Kama Sutra of Vatsyayana. Edited, with preface, by W. G. Archer. George Allen & Unwin, London. 1963

Kama Sutra. Panther Books, London. 1963

ALEX COMFORT. *The Koka Shastra*. George Allen & Unwin, London. 1964

P. Y. DESHPANDE. *Patanjali's Yoga Sutra*. Hutchinson/Rider, London. 1978

ROMESH C. DUTT. *Ramayana*. Orient, Bombay. Undated

GEORGE KEYT. *Gita Govinda, Song of Love*. Hind, Delhi. Undated

R. E. LATHAM. *De Rerum Natura of Lucretius*. Penguin, London. 1951

MAHARISHI MAHESH YOGI. *Bhagavad Gita*. Penguin, London. 1969

J. MASCARO. *Bhagavad Gita*. Penguin, London. 1962

J. L. MASSON and D. D. KOSAMBY. *Avimaraka*. Motilal Banarsidas, Delhi. 1970

R. P. OLIVER. *The Little Clay Cart*. Edited by H. W. Wells. Asia Publishing House, New York. 1964

R. S. PANDIT. *Ritusamhara of Kalidasa*. Chetana, Bombay. 1947

C. RAJAGOPALACHARI. *Mahabharata*. Bharatiya Vidhya Bhavan, Bombay. 1966

A. SHEARER and P. RUSSELL. *The Upanishads*. Wildwood House, London. 1978

S. C. UPADHYAYA. *Vatsyayana's Kama Sutra*. Taraporevala, Bombay. 1961

R. C. ZAEHNER. *Hindu Scriptures*. J. M. Dent, London. 1966

History and Literary History

A. L. BASHAM. *The Wonder That Was India*. Sidgwick & Jackson, London. 1954

N. N. BHATTACHARYA. *History of Indian Erotic Literature*. Munshiram Manoharlal, New Delhi. 1975

S. K. DE. *Ancient Indian Erotics and Erotic Literature*. Firma K. L. Mukhopadhyay, Calcutta. 1969

J. J. MEYER. *Sexual Life in Ancient India*. 2 vols. Motilal Banarsidas, Delhi. 1971

J. TOD. *Annals and Antiquities of Rajasthan*. 2 vols. M. N. Publishers, New Delhi. 1968

Yoga and Tantra

B. K. S. IYENGAR. *Light on Yoga*. George Allen & Unwin, London. 1966

R. LANNOY and H. BAINES. *The Eye of Love*. Hutchinson/Rider, London. 1976

N. P. PANDIT. *Lights on the Tantra*. Ganesh & Co, Madras. 1971

PHILIP RAWSON. *The Art of Tantra*. Thames & Hudson, London. 1973

MALCOLM STRUTT. *Living Yoga*. Centre Community Publications, London. 1976

GUISEPPE TUCCI. *Rati Lila*. Nagel, Geneva. 1969

ERNEST WOOD. *Yoga*. Penguin, London. 1959

General

JOHN ALLEGRO. *The Sacred Mushroom and the Cross*. Hodder & Stoughton, London. 1970

A. DANIELOU. *The Ragas of Northern Indian Music*. Barrie & Cresset, London. 1968

H. DAVENPORT. *Udaipur*. Maharana of Mewar Foundation, Udaipur. 1975

JAWAHARLAL NEHRU. *The Discovery of India*. Anchor, New York. 1960

S. D. PUNEKAR and KAMALA RAO. *A Study of Prostitutes in Bombay*. Lalvani, Bombay. 1962

RADHAKRISHNAN *The Hindu View of Life*. Unwin, London. 1927

IDRIES SHAH. *Oriental Magic*. Rider, London. 1956

P. THOMAS. *Kama Katha*. Taraporevala, Bombay. 1969

Reference

V. S. APTE. *Sanskrit-English Dictionary*. Motilal Banarsidas, Delhi. 1968

S. C. BANERJI. *Aspects of Ancient Indian Life from Sanskrit Sources*. Punthi Pustaka, Calcutta. 1972

J. F. DASTUR. *Medicinal Plants of India and Pakistan*. Taraporevala, Bombay. 1962

Useful Plants of India and Pakistan. Taraporevala, Bombay. 1964

Encyclopaedia Britannica. Chicago. 1979 edition

V. IONS. *Indian Mythology*. Hamlyn, London. 1967

H. E. L. MELLERSH. *Chronology of the Ancient World*. Barrie & Jenkins, London. 1976

SIR MONIER MONIER-WILLIAMS. *Sanskrit-English Dictionary*. Oxford. 1964 edition

A. M. SHASTRI. *India as seen in the Kuttani-Mata of Damodara Gupta*. Motilal Banarsidas, Delhi. 1975

A. REEJSINGHANI. *Delights from Maharashtra*. A cookery book. Jaico, Bombay. 1975

Painting and Sculpture

F. S. AIJAZUDDIN. *Pahari Paintings and Sikh Portraits*. Philip Wilson, London. 1977

MULK RAJ ANAND (Ed.). *Konarak*. Marg Publications, Bombay. 1968

D. BARRETT and B. GRAY. *Indian Painting*. Macmillan, London. 1978

J. BHRIJBHUSHAN. *The World of Indian Miniatures*. Kodansha, Tokyo. 1979

M. BUSSAGLI. *Indian Miniatures*. Macmillan, London. 1976

TOBY FALK. *Indian Painting*. Colnaghi, London. 1978

TOBY FALK and SIMON DIGBY. *Paintings from Mughal India*. Colnaghi, London. 1979

O. C. GANGULY. *Critical Catalogue of Miniature Paintings in the Baroda Museum*. Mankad, Baroda. 1961

A. GAUR. *Writing Materials of the East*. British Library, London. 1979

AJIT MOOKERJEE. *Yoga Art*. Thames & Hudson, London. 1975

N. S. RANDHAWA. *Kangra Valley Paintings*. Government of India, New Delhi. 1954

Basohli Painting. Government of India, New Delhi. 1959

Kangra Paintings on Love. National Museum, New Delhi. 1962

Kangra Ragamala Paintings. National Museum, New Delhi. 1971

PHILIP RAWSON. *Erotic Art of India*. Thames & Hudson, London. 1977

R. REIFF. *Oriental Miniatures*. Souvenir Press, London. 1965

B. W. ROBINSON. *Persian and Mughal Art*. Colnaghi, London. 1976

L. SHIVESHWARKAR. *Chaurapanchasika*. National Museum, New Delhi. 1967

A. WATTS. *Erotic Spirituality, a vision of Konarak*. Collier, London. 1971

S. C. WELCH. *Imperial Mughal Painting*. Chatto & Windus, London. 1978

ACKNOWLEDGEMENTS

Firstly, I would like to express my gratitude to my wife, Vickie, who researched the pictures and encouraged me at every stage. Together we would like to thank the following people and institutions for their help in preparing this book: Professor Suresh Upadhyaya of Bharatiya Vidhya Bhavan, Bombay, for interpreting difficult passages in Vatsyayana's text; my father, Captain Bhagwati Prasad Sinha, for his hospitality during our researches in India, and for his valuable insights into *yoga* philosophy and *Bhagavad Gita*, and my mother Mrs Liz Phare-Sinha for opening many doors to us in India, and for much of the information in the footnotes.

Dr Mulk Raj Anand, Shirrin Anand and Dolly Sahiar of Marg Magazine were immensely generous with advice and introductions to art experts in Bombay and elsewhere. Mr Vincent Phillips of Lonavla was a mine of information about Maharashtrian tribal customs. C. L. Bharani, H. S. Hiran, the poet Ram Charan Sharma 'Vyakul' of Jaipur, the Udaipur painter Bhrij Mohan Mundra and others explained and allowed us to photograph their beautiful paintings. We are most grateful to Sharad Apte for his photography in the Prince of Wales Museum, Bombay and to Shri Bhupendra Ratansi of Bombay for his knowledgeable advice about Bharata's *Natyashastra*. Our thanks are also due to Shri S. V. Gorakshkar and Shridhar Andhare of the Prince of Wales Museum of Western India, Bombay; Shri S. K. Bhowmik and Shri M. N. Gandhi of the Baroda Museum; Professor A. L. Jani and the staff of the Oriental Institute, Baroda; Dr Asko Kumar Das of the Maharaja Sawai Man Singh II Museum, Jaipur, and Shri O. P. Sharma of the National Museum New Delhi, who all gave freely of their time and expert knowledge.

The staff of the Victoria and Albert Museum, London, helped us enormously, as did Colnaghi Ltd, London. I am most grateful to the staff of the British Library's Oriental Reading Room, who patiently tracked down several obscure texts for me, and to Shreeram Vidhyarthi of London, who was a constant source of material and encouragement.

I would also like to thank Sidgwick & Jackson Ltd, London, for permission to quote from A. L. Basham's *The Wonder That Was India*, and Penguin Books Ltd, Harmondsworth, England, for permission to quote a verse from Professor John Brough's *Poems From The Sanskrit*, and Jamila Bhrijbhushan from whose outstanding and brilliant book *The World Of Indian Miniatures* I culled much of the information about Indian painting given in the Introduction.

Our special thanks to Victor Lownes, who allowed us to ransack his house and reproduce many fine paintings from his unique collection.

Finally, our thanks to Lance Dane, who generously put his enormous collection of paintings and photographs at our disposal, despite the fact that he was himself bringing out an illustrated edition of Burton's *Kama Sutra*. Lance's thirty years as a photographer of Indian art have enabled him to illustrate his book with a wealth of material, making it a virtual encyclopaedia of Indian erotic art.

Whether or not it is the fashion, I should also like to thank my editors at London Editions, Rosalie Vicars-Harris and Diana Mansour, who have had a difficult and unenviable task coping with this mass of unfamiliar material, and with an all too often fractious author.

PICTURE CREDITS